W9-CVA-792

Outcasts on Main Street

Report of the
Federal
Task Force on
Homelessness and
Severe Mental Illness

February, 1992

The Honorable Jack Kemp
Secretary of Housing and Urban Development
Chairman, Interagency Council on the Homeless
Washington, D.C. 20410

The Honorable Louis Sullivan, M.D.
Secretary of Health and Human Services
Vice-Chairman, Interagency Council on the Homeless
Washington, D.C. 20410

Dear Secretary Kemp and Secretary Sullivan:

We, the members of the Task Force on Homelessness and Severe Mental Illness, which you convened in May 1990, are delighted to share with you and the Interagency Council on the Homeless the results of our deliberations during the past 18 months. Aided by a very active and dedicated Advisory Committee, as well as a broad range of concerned individuals and organizations who have shared their knowledge and opinions with us, we have developed a national strategy and specific action steps designed to end homelessness among people with severe mental illnesses.

The Task Force members are all representatives of Federal departments that are directly involved in efforts to improve the lives of homeless people, including those who have severe mental illnesses. We have outlined specific ways our respective departments, coordinating and targeting our efforts, can do even more, and do it better.

The goal of ending homelessness among mentally ill people ultimately will be achieved locally as people work in their own neighborhoods, communities, and towns to help their less fortunate neighbors obtain stable housing and services and rejoin the community as contributing members. Recognizing that fact, we have developed a *national* rather than a *Federal* plan of action. We view our role as providing leadership in a process that involves not only the Federal Government, but also State and local governments, working in concert with many people in the private and voluntary sectors.

Our deliberations have focused on responding to the special needs and characteristics of the estimated one-third of the homeless, single adult population who suffer from severe mental illnesses. However, we believe that many of the lessons we have learned and the approaches we recommend may be applicable to other segments of both the homeless and the mentally ill populations. We therefore offer this report in the hope that, through our collective efforts, task forces and councils concerned with homelessness--and homelessness itself--will become a thing of the past.

Respectfully,

Alan I. Leshner, Ph.D., Chair
Task Force on Homelessness
and Severe Mental Illness
Acting Director
National Institute of Mental Health

Table of Contents

Acknowledgments

The members of the Task Force on Homelessness and Severe Mental Illness have received invaluable assistance and contributions from hundreds of individuals and organizations—far more than we can acknowledge by name here. Many of those to whom we are most indebted are listed in the appendix.

We owe a special debt of gratitude to our Advisory Committee. Its 16 members have generously shared with us their practical experience, their wisdom, and their visions of a better life for homeless people with severe mental illnesses. We have attempted to incorporate and reflect their sage advice, but responsibility for the substance of this report rests solely with the Task Force.

We are also grateful to the individuals and organizations who provided program descriptions and case reports of homeless severely mentally ill individuals for background use. In particular, our appreciation extends to Carol Caton, Kim Hopper, David Pendergast, Russell Schutt, and Miles Shore for contributions to the composite vignettes (with details changed to protect privacy) presented in our report.

Photo ©MAUREEN FENNELLI
Also appearing in the National Mental Health Association's *Homeless in America* (1988).

Executive Summary

Dressed in a makeshift uniform, James Lee stands at attention in front of the train station, shouting orders at an invisible platoon. His uniform looks neat, but he is filthy, he smells, and there are open sores on his legs. Sometimes passersby toss change into the helmet at his feet. Diagnosed as having schizophrenia, James marches to a drummer inside his head. The pavement he guards is his home.

The outreach worker met Scarlet McCaffrey outside the library. Scarlet looks somewhat scholarly, but she is not studying. She carries a stack of books in one arm, a threadbare bed roll in the other. She rarely talks; at times she'll drink from a flask hidden in her layers of clothes. The outreach worker remarked, "She won't give us a date of birth, her Social Security number, or any other information; we just can't get a history."

Benjamin Draper rides the subway all day. Dressed neatly and cleanly, he scribbles on a legal pad, creating pages of intricate doodles and repeated words and patterns. Underground he feels safe; above ground, he wears a bicycle helmet to protect his thoughts from interfering radio waves. He always carries his medication with him, but won't take any; he is afraid the pills are poisoned.

These scenes from a human tragedy are an increasingly familiar and disturbing part of the American landscape. Every winter the plight of homeless people is discovered anew by the media, and people of goodwill resolve to conquer homelessness. Researchers measure and describe it. Commissions and policymakers ponder, decry, and plan to eradicate it. Volunteers and government agencies offer food, clothing, and temporary shelter. But by the time another holiday season has arrived, our Nation is once again shocked by the presence of homeless individuals on our streets and in our parks.

We, the members of the Task Force on Homelessness and Severe Mental Illness, believe the fate of all homeless Americans *can and must* change for the better. We offer a strategy for making it happen for one of the most needy and vulnerable segments of the homeless population: those who are afflicted with severe mental illnesses. Our strategy is characterized by thoughtfully planned action, not quick fixes. Therefore, we expect the impact of our work to be pervasive and long-lasting.

In response to our charge from the Interagency Council on the Homeless, we offer over 50 action steps that Federal Departments participating in the Task Force will take to end homelessness among severely mentally ill individuals. These steps are intended to improve substantially this country's system of care and housing options for homeless mentally ill persons by making essential resources, both traditional and novel, more accessible to these disabled Americans. In addition, we present recommendations to State and local governments and the private sector to encourage their necessary leadership in helping this beleaguered group of individuals escape from homelessness.

The roadmap presented in this report is one we believe can take our Nation a long way toward ending homelessness among people with severe mental illness. And if we can do it for them, we can do it for anyone. Here are our major findings, recommendations, and action steps.

Homeless and Severely Mentally Ill People: Who Are They and Why Are They Homeless?

On any given night, up to 600,000 people are literally homeless, living and sleeping on our streets, in parks, in shelters, or in darkened corners of public transportation settings. About one-third of these homeless, single adults are suffering from severe mental illnesses such as schizophrenia or manic-depressive disorder. Untreated, their disorders fog thoughts, sap motivation, and can turn emotions into engines of terror, rage, or despair. Severe mental illnesses and their attendant disabilities may be life-long and recurring, with symptoms waxing and waning. They affect virtually every aspect of life, including self-care, money management, schooling, work, family, and social relations. But most of the disturbing and debilitating symptoms associated with severe mental illnesses can be managed through ongoing treatment and rehabilitation in the community.

Homeless people who are severely mentally ill suffer from many additional burdens that exacerbate their illnesses and contribute to and sustain their homelessness. In the forefront of these are the lack of an adequate income, diminished social supports, and the frequent presence of alcohol and/or other drug abuse problems. Other critical contributing factors include the lack of affordable and appropriate housing, the fragmentation of service systems for people with severe mental illnesses, community resistance and discrimination, and resource limitations.

Outreach and treatment efforts for homeless members of racial and ethnic minority groups are often hampered by cultural and language barriers. In addition, many mentally ill individuals, once housed, often lack adequate supports to sustain community living and prevent another episode of homelessness.

Escaping From Homelessness: What Is Needed?

Any attempt to help people with severe mental illnesses escape from homelessness needs to address and improve all aspects of their life situation. A responsive service system must encompass and integrate an enormous range of diverse services and systems, many of which do not usually work together. Severely mentally ill individuals, in particular, cannot negotiate a service system in which health care, mental health and substance abuse treatment, social services and income support, legal services, housing, and rehabilitation and employment services are separate and uncoordinated. In addition to being comprehensive and integrated, the system of care we are promoting must be accessible to and easily maneuvered by its intended users.

There is surprisingly widespread agreement on the essential elements in such a system.

Assertive Outreach

Service providers must break out of the mold of traditional service provision and meet and engage homeless individuals on their own terms and on their own turf. By offering patient, persistent, and continuing contacts over relatively long periods of time, outreach workers can establish the trusting relationships that are essential to engage and help mentally ill people living on the street.

Integrated Care Management

Clients need an individual or team to help identify service needs and resources, to arrange for continuity of care, and to ensure the efficacy and accountability of service provision.

Safe Havens

Mentally ill people on streets or in shelters need a secure, clean, and stable residence where they can recuperate from the harsh street environment and develop necessary life skills and linkages to benefits, treatment, and supports. Unlike most shelters, these *safe havens* should place few demands on their guests and offer a place to stay during the day, the same bed each night, and storage of belongings. Additionally, individuals would be permitted to stay until appropriate housing and support services are identified.

Housing

For this population, housing is essential but not sufficient; it must be coordinated with services that can help individuals remain housed. Given the extreme poverty of the population, a variety of housing options must be made affordable through a range or combination of approaches, including greater access to housing subsidies and increased employment opportunities.

Treatment of Mental Illness

All people with severe mental illnesses—including those who are home-less—require ongoing access to a full range of treatment and rehabilitation services to lessen symptoms as well as the impairment and disruption they produce. Most homeless mentally ill people do not need hospitalization, and even fewer require long-term institutional care. But for those who do require occasional hospitalization, hospital discharge policies should ensure continuity of treatment and care as well as provision of appropriate housing, benefits, and supports upon release.

Alcohol and/or Other Drug Abuse Treatment

At least half of the homeless severely mentally ill population also suffer from alcohol and/or other drug abuse problems. These dually diagnosed people require skilled assessment and access to detoxification, treatment, and recovery services (e.g., counseling, referral, self-help services) specifically designed to deal with co-occurring problems, as well as specialized residential services.

Health Care

Unattended health problems of the target population commonly range from life-threatening infectious diseases such as acquired immunodeficiency syndrome (AIDS) and tuberculosis to less serious disorders that interact with or complicate the diagnosis and/or treatment of their mental illnesses. Homelessness makes effective treatment of even minor conditions difficult, significantly shortening the lifespan of these citizens. These people must have access to the full range of medical and dental assessment, diagnosis, treatment, and prevention.

Income Support and Benefits

Homeless mentally ill people must receive outreach and assistance to ensure that they obtain and retain all entitlements and benefits for which they are eligible. Key income-support programs include Supplemental Security Income (SSI), Social Security Disability Insurance (SSDI), Aid to Families with Dependent Children, food stamps, State general assistance, local welfare assistance, and veterans benefits.

Rehabilitation, Vocational Training, and Employment Assistance

Severely mentally ill people who have been homeless need to develop or relearn social skills and competencies as well as work skills. Key services include: assessment of goals, skills, and supports; linkage with vocational training, jobs, and other meaningful daytime activities; and opportunities to participate in supported employment, clubhouse programs, self-help programs, and recreational activities.

Consumer and Family Involvement

Both consumers of mental health services and families of people with severe mental illnesses are potentially valuable but often overlooked allies in service provision. Consumer-run programs for the target population should be encouraged, as should supports that enable families with mentally ill members to provide needed housing and care when such an arrangement is mutually desirable.

Legal Protections

People who are severely mentally ill and homeless need legal protections from many types of abuse, mistreatment, and discrimination. Services must be available to protect client and patient rights, to advocate (both at the individual and systems levels) for improved access to appropriate housing and care, and to promote consumer empowerment and choice.

Steps in Support of Improved Service Delivery

In addition to the essential components outlined above, improved services for the severely mentally ill homeless population require:

- ongoing research to provide more precise information about what works, for whom, and under what circumstances;

- community education to enhance public understanding and acceptance of severely mentally ill homeless individuals in housing settings and the workplace; and

- educational activities to retrain existing service workers and to provide new workers with the necessary knowledge, skills, and attitudes to work with the homeless mentally ill population.

How Can the Federal Government Help to End Homelessness Among People With Severe Mental Illnesses?

There is no single, simple solution to the problems of homelessness among the mentally ill population across our Nation. Any successful effort to end their homelessness must be a pluralistic one, involving Federal, State, and local governments as well as providers, mental health consumers, family members, and voluntary organizations. Each community must discover and develop the most effective configuration of resources to meet its own needs.

To ease and hasten this process of discovery, we, the members of the Task Force on Homelessness and Severe Mental Illness, have developed action steps to address four main goals: promoting systems integration, expanding housing options and alternative services, improving outreach efforts and access to existing programs, and generating and disseminating knowledge and information.

While solutions to this problem must be multifaceted, our emphasis on the Federal role reflects our special expertise as well as our belief that appropriate Federal leadership can stimulate the changes required to end homelessness among severely mentally ill people in America. Recommendations for non-Federal organizations are also provided. A sampling of the Federal action steps is presented below.

Promote Systems Integration: The ACCESS Initiative

There is growing consensus that a truly integrated system of care for people who are homeless and severely mentally ill requires integrating basic life supports (e.g., food, clothing, and shelter) with specialized services (e.g., treatment); linking services at the client and system levels; coordinating Federal, State, and local resources; and providing a clear delineation of authority and of clinical, fiscal, and administrative responsibility. For most communities in the United States, services integration is more an ideal than a reality. Thus, the Task Force sought to develop new incentives to help communities explore ways to make this integration happen.

- The Department of Health and Human Services (HHS), in collaboration with the Department of Housing and Urban Development (HUD), the Department of Labor (DOL), the Department of Education (DOEd), the Department of Veterans Affairs (VA), and the Department of Agriculture (USDA), will make *Access to Community Care and Effective Services and Supports (ACCESS)* grants available to the States.

  This innovative interdepartmental effort will test promising approaches to services integration within 20 to 30 communities selected to receive immediate assistance in ending homelessness among severely mentally ill individuals. The Federal Government will provide extensive pre- and post-award technical assistance to help each community take full advantage of available resources and offer expedited review of waiver requests and eligibility claims.

Other action steps to promote systems integration include:

- HHS (National Institute of Mental Health—NIMH) and the Department of Justice will develop a Memorandum of Understanding to stimulate approaches to divert to appropriate treatment settings those homeless people with severe mental illnesses who are inappropriately placed in jails.

- The Departments of Labor, HHS, and Education will establish a Memorandum of Understanding to guide collaborative efforts to address knowledge gaps and stimulate policy and program development in meeting the rehabilitation and job training needs of the homeless mentally ill population.

Expand Housing Options and Alternative Services: Safe Havens

Despite widespread agreement that homeless people with severe mental illnesses need the types of safe havens described above, few now exist. The Task Force will undertake the following to fill this void in the service system:

- HUD will propose to Congress a new, competitive demonstration program of safe havens designed to determine the feasibility of providing low-cost stable housing for homeless mentally ill (and homeless dually diagnosed) people living on the street.

  This expanded housing option is intended to meet the needs of people who are initially reluctant to participate in structured programs. It offers a low-demand environment that provides safety, security, supervision, and support; and will be more stable than shelters because residents can use the same bed each night and are not forced to leave. These facilities will provide opportunities for residents to establish ties to treatment, benefits, and other support services.

  Support would be provided for the rehabilitation and operating costs of safe havens. Grants would be awarded competitively and would include operating costs for a 5-year period, with the possibility of renewal in future years.

Additional steps to expand housing options and alternative services include:

- The HUD Shelter Plus Care (S+C) program provides flexible rental assistance for a wide array of living arrangements including single-room-occupancy (SRO) units, group homes, and individual apartments. HUD is seeking congressional approval to reprogram funds for the Tenant Rental Assistance component of the Shelter Plus Care Program in 1992, and will seek full funding for 1993.

- To simplify administration of the S+C program, HUD will recommend to Congress amendment of the McKinney Act so that the existing three components of the program would be folded into one offering three types of rental assistance—tenant-based, project-based, and sponsor-based—which will provide more flexibility and responsiveness to local needs and conditions.

Improve Outreach and Access to Existing Programs

A major finding of the Task Force has been the recognition that existing Federal programs and benefits relevant—and often essential—to homeless people with severe mental illnesses are not being fully utilized. Among the measures we propose to overcome these problems and ensure that Federal programs reach their intended target populations are:

- HHS (Social Security Administration—SSA) will continue to increase out-reach activities to homeless individuals, especially to homeless mentally ill persons. SSA will do this in part through its SSI outreach demonstration projects. These projects seek to demonstrate effective, efficient, ongoing, and transferable approaches for identifying potentially eligible individuals, assisting them through the application process, helping them to continue to receive SSI benefits as long as they remain eligible, and linking them with other available and appropriate financial benefits and social services. These efforts, including a special joint SSA-VA initiative, are directed at improving the quality of their lives and helping them obtain the greatest possible measure of independence.

- A basic component of the VA Homeless Chronically Mentally Ill (HCMI) Veterans Program is assertive outreach to homeless mentally ill veterans in shelters, at soup kitchens, and on the streets. The VA will expand outreach to local homelessness coalitions and nonprofit organizations at its HCMI and Domiciliary Care for Homeless Veterans Program sites.

Generate and Disseminate Knowledge and Information

Substantial resources, both public and private, are available to improve the lives of homeless people, including those who are severely mentally ill. However, many communities, service providers, and eligible individuals are not making use of them—especially those offered by the Federal Government—because they are unaware that such resources are available. The following action steps are designed to address critical information gaps and promote the coordination required to close them:

- HHS (Alcohol, Drug Abuse, and Mental Health Administration—ADAMHA) will undertake a national community education initiative to educate the public about the homeless population with co-occurring alcohol, drug, and mental health disorders. This initiative will include research and research demonstration programs as well as dissemination of information through publications and conferences.

- HHS (NIMH and Office for Treatment Improvement, ADAMHA) will fund an integrated treatment center to assess the efficacy of this approach in treating homeless mentally ill persons with co-occurring alcohol and/or other drug disorders. Comprehensive psychosocial and psychiatric assessments, together with appropriate medical interventions, would be supported through a central intake, assessment, and referral unit. Housing, vocational rehabilitation, and other essential elements of an integrated system of care would be ensured.

- HHS (NIMH) will identify exemplary comprehensive projects that integrate housing and support services for homeless severely mentally ill persons and will disseminate information on how they were developed and how they can be adapted to other communities. NIMH will expand dissemination activities of the National Resource Center on Homelessness and Mental Illness, which is co-funded by NIMH and HUD, to assist housing, treatment, and service providers in addressing the needs of the target population.

Provide Continuing Oversight: Role of the Interagency Council on the Homeless

A sustained effort is required to address the complex factors that cause and prolong homelessness among people with severe mental illnesses. Therefore, we have recommended, and the Interagency Council on the Homeless has agreed, that the Council will develop, within 60 days from the issuance of this report, a plan for monitoring and tracking the completion of each of the Federal action steps outlined in the report and for identifying new opportunities to assist States and localities in meeting the needs of their homeless mentally ill citizens.

Additionally, a committee of the Council, working closely with NIMH and other agencies, will be constituted to provide integrated Federal leadership and oversight to address the needs of homeless severely mentally ill people on an ongoing basis.

Conclusion

For thousands of Americans with severe mental illnesses, homelessness is the final indignity in a life of pain, poverty, and unfulfilled promise. Our Task Force has outlined a way our Nation can begin to turn around these tragic circumstances and respond to the best prompting of our own national conscience. It says clearly: *This is a problem we can and must solve together. The time to begin is now.*

Photo © ABRAHAM MENASHE
Also appearing in the National Mental Health Association's *Homeless in America* (1988).

Prologue

THIS IS A REPORT ABOUT HELPING PEOPLE WITH MENTAL ILLNESSES WHO HAVE NO PLACE TO CALL HOME

Studies have shown that about one out of every three homeless people in the United States suffers from a severe mental illness, such as schizophrenia or manic-depressive illness (Tessler and Dennis 1989). The plight of these individuals represents a singular challenge for their communities and for the Nation at large. For any homeless person, poverty and the stresses of street life increase the difficulty of keeping body, mind, and spirit well. But for those also burdened with severe mental illnesses, the task becomes overwhelming. For any homeless person, the path out of homelessness is often long and paved with difficulties and setbacks. But for those with severe mental illnesses, there may be no pathway at all, or it may repeatedly lead back to the streets—as it did for a young man we will call "Michael Dodge."

Michael Dodge is dead. He hurled himself through a third-story window and fell into the parking lot of a fast food restaurant. It was his fifth suicide attempt in 10 years, and unfortunately, it worked.

He had been a delicate, withdrawn child. He and his sister Elizabeth were moved from one small Southwestern town to the next as their father sought oil-drilling work. Michael was never able to establish a secure footing for schooling or friendship. His mother died when he was 17, and his father's grief was profound and prolonged. Soon after, Michael began to experience deep fears about strangers reading his mind or his journal and stealing his ideas.

Elizabeth then took him to live with her when she moved to the East Coast. But drug problems and violence were rampant in the few neighborhoods she could afford to live in. Because of Michael's shyness and peculiar ideas, his only "friends" were the neighborhood's addicts and prostitutes, who usually conned him out of his money. "Still," he once said, "they're better than nobody." Elizabeth, at one point, convinced Michael to get treatment, and he reluctantly agreed to see someone at the local mental health center. The psychiatrist Michael met with was concerned about his disorganized thinking and recommended a brief hospital stay for medical tests. Michael refused. The psychiatrist prescribed antipsychotic medication, which Michael took for a couple of days. But then Michael stopped the medication, saying, "It feels like poison," and refused to return to the clinic.

1

Despite his deepening psychosis and depression, Michael searched out jobs, but no employer could keep him for long. He tried working in an all-night gas station but found it difficult to stay awake and concentrate on making change. He tried stuffing envelopes for an insurance company but was fired for being too slow.

Michael had a major blowup with Elizabeth over his refusal to shower or bathe. They also argued over the elaborate "security measures" Michael insisted that Elizabeth obey upon entering the apartment. Michael said they were necessary to protect his thoughts. After the yelling, Michael picked up his few possessions, walked out the door, and began living on the streets. He spent his days quietly writing in his journal and searching for food since he was too shy to panhandle. He avoided Elizabeth and ignored her urging to return to the apartment. Then, late one night, Michael was raped in an alley. He was so humiliated that he swallowed a whole bottle of acetaminophen and was rushed to a municipal hospital—just in time.

Many other suicide attempts occurred during the next 3 years while Michael rotated through shelters, halfway houses, abandoned buildings, and hobo camps. Ending his life became a preoccupation, and in his darkest periods, he heard voices imploring suicide.

Michael's disability payments were often delayed or lost because he had no permanent address or was hospitalized, but no one seemed concerned or took responsibility for the situation. Indeed, in the 10 years that Michael wandered the streets, tens of thousands of dollars were spent on ambulances and emergency interventions, but he never received the assistance he needed in finding effective treatment, appropriate housing, or work.

A few days before his 28th birthday, after being laid off again, Michael jumped out of the window of an abandoned apartment building. His body was cremated by the city government, and Elizabeth claimed the ashes a few months later.

No person in our country should ever experience the long-term destitution, despair, and demoralization of someone like Michael. In the belief that our Nation *can and must* do far better, the Task Force on Homelessness and Severe Mental Illness was charged with finding more effective ways for the Federal Government, States, and local organizations, both public and private, to meet the housing, treatment, and support needs of this extremely poor and disabled population.

In response to this charge, we have developed a plan of action designed to make stories like Michael's obsolete. The plan puts forth a strategy for enhancing access to housing, treatment, and other support services for people with severe mental illnesses and helping them escape from homelessness while encouraging their autonomy and independence in the community.

Because of the great complexity and multifaceted nature of the problem of homelessness among severely mentally ill people, its solution will not occur instantaneously. Nor will it happen through the actions—no matter how committed—of any single segment of the country's very pluralistic and diverse systems of care. We offer a vision of what the ideal care system for this population should look like. We have also specified beginning action steps that we in the Federal Government will take to make that vision a reality, coupled with recommendations for complementary actions by other levels of government and the private sector. By working together systematically, we will hasten the day when we reach our mutual goal: ending homelessness among people with severe mental illnesses.

We are encouraged that many communities across the country have already shown that it is possible to develop a broad range of treatment, housing, and support options for severely mentally ill people who are homeless or at risk of being homeless. They have found ways to pull together and sustain the complex array of supportive services—social, economic, medical, and rehabilitative—essential to successful adaptation to community living. The story of Gladys Williams took place in one such community:

> Gladys Williams says her right hand is crooked because a policeman shot her years ago when she pulled out a toy pistol; she was just high and having some fun. The doctors at the charity hospital patched up her hand as best they could, but it was a mess, and so was her life. After the shooting she took to the streets, as she often did in times of trouble. Somewhere along the way she had stopped taking her medications, and the voices returned that had haunted her intermittently for decades. They warned her to move on because people were after her who would freeze her to death.

> Gladys didn't like the shelters (and she had tried them all over the years), but one bitter cold night a few years ago, she tried out a new shelter a young street worker had recommended. After a few weeks there, Gladys started a fight with the woman in the next cot, who, she believed, was sending her messages through the television. Most shelters simply sent Gladys back on the streets when she got into fights, but this one was different; they sent her to a mental health center, where she was assessed and treated as an inpatient for a while.

> The medications silenced the voices, and she started to feel better. After a few weeks, when she was ready to leave the hospital, her case manager arranged for her to move temporarily to the center's specialized residence for homeless mentally ill people. By now, Gladys, working with her case manager, was able to start attending to the rest of her life—what she called "the gettings": getting someplace decent to live, getting good medical care (including surgery to make her hand more usable), getting off alcohol and other drugs, and getting some education and training so she could get a paid job instead of living on welfare, but she also talked about "the givings": using her considerable street wisdom and native intelligence to help other people.

3

During the next few years, Gladys, with the support of many other people, gradually accomplished most of her gettings and givings. She moved into Hilltop Inn, a small residence of 16 units, owned and operated by the mental health center. There she had her own sunny room and, assisted by a resident manager, shared with other residents the duties of running the household.

She regained most of the use of her hand after an eminent orthopedic surgeon at a local teaching hospital agreed to operate free of charge, through the help and strong advocacy of center staff. She participated regularly in the many programs offered by the mental health center—including therapy, medication management, job skills training, and the social club—and grew closer to the people she met at Alcoholics Anonymous meetings, Hilltop Inn, and the mental health center.

Just this year she was elected president of the social club and received a regional award for her outstanding work as a volunteer at a neighborhood soup kitchen. In accepting the social club presidency, Gladys summed up her recent past this way:

> *Friends at the mental health center have made the difference in the last few years. It is nice to recognize faces in the world, to be part of something, and to be acknowledged and recognized. I struggle hard to be a good person and to stay a good person; I want to show people that their faith in me has not been misplaced. Now I am fighting for my right to live and survive and be in my own decent place. I am still working to improve my situation by looking for better housing and am currently on a couple of waiting lists. Now I want to forget the past because I feel I've gone beyond it.*

The simple reality is this: Many outcomes are possible for the severely mentally ill people now on our Nation's streets. The stories of Michael and Gladys represent two divergent outcomes. Each of us must choose how we as a Nation want this story to end.

Task Force on Homelessness And Severe Mental Illness

The Task Force on Homelessness and Severe Mental Illness was convened by the Interagency Council on the Homeless, which, under the guidance of its Chairman, Jack Kemp, Secretary of Housing and Urban Development, and its Vice Chairman, Dr. Louis W. Sullivan, Secretary of Health and Human Services, is responsible for coordinating all Federal activities concerning the homeless population. The Task Force consists of representatives from all major Federal departments whose policies and programs directly affect the homeless severely mentally ill population.

We, the members of the Task Force, have been guided in our deliberations by a 16-member Advisory Committee appointed by Dr. Sullivan, which includes experts in diverse fields ranging from mental health research to housing administration. Citizen advocates and mental health consumers are represented, as well as State and local officials concerned with severe mental illnesses and homelessness.

In addition, we have made extensive efforts to reach out to relevant non-Federal organizations and groups to solicit information and guidance. In mid-June 1991, a letter of inquiry was sent to nearly 20,000 individuals and organizations throughout the Nation soliciting advice and recommendations. The responses to this letter were carefully read and analyzed. A series of workshops was convened with groups of experts on topics central to the Task Force charge including clinical, housing, minority, consumer, rehabilitation, and legal issues and concerns. Finally, Task Force members participated in a public hearing on severe mental illness and homelessness held September 5, 1991, in Chicago, Illinois. The hearing, which was jointly sponsored by the National Advisory Mental Health Council and the National Mental Health Leadership Forum, resulted in relevant testimony from numerous individuals and organizations around the country, which we also considered.

In the pages to follow, we present a plan of action that we believe reflects a vital first step toward ending homelessness among people with severe mental illnesses.

- We have outlined fundamental principles as well as the essential components of an integrated and comprehensive system of care for homeless people with severe mental illnesses.

- We have initiated immediate action steps and identified more long-term systemic measures that our own Federal departments can and will take to facilitate State and local efforts.

- We have proposed new opportunities for States and communities to develop, test, and improve the organization, financing, and delivery of a wide range of essential services for homeless people with severe mental illnesses.

- We have recommended steps that States and local organizations can take to respond more appropriately to the needs of severely mentally ill homeless people.

We are delighted to share our findings and recommendations with the Interagency Council on the Homeless and are grateful for the opportunity to offer a new perspective on one of the most disabled and needy subgroups of the homeless population. The Council is performing a crucial role by helping States and localities address broad housing, economic, and social welfare issues related to the complex problem of homelessness in America. Any efforts to assist the broader homeless population will certainly benefit those among them with severe mental illnesses. Conversely, the knowledge and encouragement gained from discovering effective ways to help the severely mentally ill segment of the homeless population will benefit all homeless persons who so desperately need our help.

Photo ©TONEE HARBERT
Also appearing in the National Mental Health Association's *Homeless in America* (1988).

The Nature of the Population

Severely Mentally Ill And Homeless People: The Target Population

On any given night, up to 600,000 Americans are literally homeless.[1] And of these homeless individuals, approximately one-third of the single adults suffer from the added burden of severe mental illnesses.[2] It is this segment of the homeless population to which this report is primarily devoted. By severe mental illnesses we refer to persistent mental or emotional disorders (including, but not limited to, schizophrenia, schizoaffective disorders, mood disorders, and severe personality disorders) that significantly interfere with a person's ability to carry out such primary aspects of daily life as self-care, household management, interpersonal relationships, and work or school.

This population has been singled out for intensive consideration by the Interagency Council on the Homeless through the interdepartmental Task Force on Homelessness and Severe Mental Illness because it represents one of the most obviously vulnerable and ill-served groups in our Nation. As if homelessness and severe mental illness were not enough, many of these individuals are also burdened by problems of substance abuse, physical illness, and the adverse consequences of extreme poverty. Further, at the point where a home is no longer available, many no longer have family relationships or friendships that might provide comfort or help.

This group of highly disadvantaged people is large enough to present a very visible and disturbing presence in many communities throughout the United States, particularly in urban areas. At the same time, this group is small

---

[1] For purposes of this report, we define a "homeless person" in keeping with the Stewart B. McKinney Homeless Assistance Act (Public Law 100–77) which, in its opening sentence, refers to homelessness as a lack of shelter. Within this context, the Act then defines a homeless person as someone "who lacks a fixed, regular, and adequate nighttime residence" and someone whose primary nighttime residence is a "supervised public or private shelter designed to provide temporary living accommodations; an institution that provides a temporary residence for individuals intended to be institutionalized; or a public or private place not designed for, or ordinarily used as, a regular sleeping accommodation for human beings." The estimated number is based on a national homeless study conducted by the Urban Institute (Burt and Cohen 1989).

[2] The prevalence of severe mental illnesses among single, homeless adults may vary across different communities (Tessler and Dennis 1989).

enough to make the goal of housing them and enabling them to establish a more settled way of life seem quite feasible.

Like other homeless people, those with severe mental illnesses are found in parks, airports, and terminals; in shelters and soup kitchens; in jails and general hospitals; and under bridges and on streets and sidewalks—in both urban and rural areas. Unlike some other homeless people, however, their chances of escaping from homelessness on their own are minuscule because the symptoms of severe mental disorders typically disrupt the very judgment, motivation, and social skills that are essential for adaptive community living.

Thus, the primary goal of the Task Force is to identify a strategy for responding more appropriately as a Nation to the complex needs of this extremely disabled group of Americans. We are particularly concerned with finding ways to increase the likelihood that, once severely mentally ill homeless people are off the streets and housed, they will remain housed and have access to necessary services and supports, regardless of changes in their clinical condition.

A secondary goal is to prevent new waves of severely mentally ill people from swelling the ranks of our country's homeless citizens. Some programs for homeless individuals distinguish between individuals who are literally homeless (as previously defined) and those who are in imminent danger of becoming homeless—a group that is much more difficult to define. Although the terms suggest that there are two distinct populations—the literally homeless and those at risk of homelessness—in fact there is considerable movement and overlap between them. Many people who lack permanent housing move through various stages and degrees of residential instability and only intermittently meet technical definitions of literal homelessness. Ending homelessness, therefore, requires efforts to keep these vulnerable individuals from ever becoming homeless and to keep formerly homeless people from having to repeat the experience.

Special Population Characteristics

Homeless adults with severe mental illnesses constitute an extremely diverse group, but most members share certain characteristics that contribute to their becoming and remaining homeless. To aid in policy development, services planning, and prevention, it is important to identify these characteristics and to identify the similarities and differences between this population and the two with which it overlaps: people who are homeless and people who have severe mental illnesses. The following brief descriptions of this population are based on research sponsored by HHS's[3] National Institute of Mental Health (NIMH) during the past decade (NIMH 1991a),

---

[3] This abbreviation and all other acronyms used in this text are listed in the appendix.

8

complemented by the extensive deliberations of the Task Force and its Advisory Committee.

Severe Mental Illnesses

The homeless people who are the focal point of this report suffer from severe mental illnesses that differ in their causes, course, and treatment. Their symptoms, too, can differ dramatically. Some people with a severe mental illness are too exhausted and overwhelmed by depression to seek the food, shelter, and medical care they desperately need; other people, equally ill, are ferociously talkative, fidgety, and wildly energized by mania. Some individuals, tortured by delusions, fantasies, suspicion, and fear, hide from any human contact; other severely mentally ill people are extremely friendly and gregarious but cannot organize their thoughts or plans. Some individuals are hostile and aggressive to the point of dangerousness; others are gentle but extremely withdrawn. The condition of homelessness itself can, of course, also exacerbate the disorientation and mistrust that often accompany severe mental illnesses.

Severe mental illnesses can be manifested in many forms, but their disabling effects are distressingly uniform: long-lasting or recurring difficulty in coping with the tasks of daily living—finding and retaining work and housing, forming and maintaining relationships, and sustaining physical and mental health. These consequences clearly have important ramifications for the design and funding of services for this population. Although severe mental disorders tend to be enduring, sometimes for life, they frequently follow a cyclical course that is unlike that of, say, mental retardation or many physical disabilities. Some people with severe mental disorders may achieve or return to extremely high levels of functioning (and competitive employment) during periods of remission.

Medications and psychosocial treatments provided on a regular basis can help many severely mentally ill people function well in community settings. In part because of dysfunctional aspects of the treatment system, many others receive little or no relief from the distressing effects of their illness. Some individuals who are difficult to treat effectively are essentially dismissed by the treatment system. Others are too disabled to maneuver the complex service system and obtain the treatment and care they need. They frequently drift out of the care system and onto the streets—undermined by the worst manifestations of these devastating, untreated disorders.

When acutely ill, some people with severe mental disorders may become totally incoherent and possibly dangerous to themselves and/or others; at such times, inpatient treatment or alternative crisis stabilization services are usually required. Although most hospital stays are brief, some people may require hospitalization for a month or more. Unfortunately, if one enters a hospital for an extended period of time, it can prove to be very difficult to retain housing or employment.

Clearly, attempts to alleviate or prevent homelessness among people with severe mental illnesses—whether by street workers and clinicians or by policymakers at the local, State, or Federal level—must be based upon an understanding of the special characteristics and long-term course of these illnesses. The service system must be both comprehensive and comprehensible; it must enable these homeless and disabled people to obtain readily what they need to function at their best.

Alcohol and/or Other Drug Abuse

For a sizable proportion of the homeless severely mentally ill population—estimated at one-half or more—the abuse of alcohol and/or other drugs often complicates their already troubled lives. For some individuals, substance abuse is a cause of homelessness; for others, it is a result. For still others it reflects an attempt at self-medication or an effort to gain peer acceptance that is causally unrelated to being homeless. For some, physical dependence on alcohol and/or other drugs demands ongoing consumption.

Whatever its origins, substance abuse by people who are severely mentally ill and homeless often makes the escape from homelessness particularly problematic. For example, many housing programs will not accept individuals with alcohol or other drug problems and will eject people who, once accepted, violate program prohibitions against use of these drugs. Alternatively, some programs require participation in alcohol or other drug treatment programs as a precondition for obtaining housing. This is a requirement some homeless people with a severe mental illness cannot satisfactorily meet for a host of reasons. They may lack the ability to access treatment independently, or the community may lack service providers capable of treating individuals who suffer from both mental illness and addictive disorders.

Clearly, major considerations for this population include providing adequate shelter and other services, even when individuals use or abuse alcohol or other drugs, and building an integrated service system in which services are available that address both mental illness and substance abuse.

Poverty

People who are homeless are among the most impoverished in our Nation, and those who are also severely mentally ill are in particularly dire straits economically. An NIMH-funded study of over 1,000 severely mentally ill people in a national sample revealed that the average income of these individuals was merely $4,200 a year. Only 25 percent of the sample were employed at all, and less than 10 percent were employed outside of sheltered workplaces (Mulkern and Manderscheid 1989), despite the fact that, as a Boston study had revealed, three-quarters of homeless respondents, with or without mental illness, wanted to work (Mulkern et al. 1985).

A study in a New York City shelter indicates that homeless people with a mental illness face more barriers to employment than do other homeless people. Such barriers include the lack of education and job skills needed to obtain permanent well-paid work—especially in a harsh economic climate (Crystal et al. 1985). Adding to these impediments is the stigmatization of this group, which makes many prospective employers reluctant to hire people with a known history of mental illness.

Severely mentally ill people are often eligible for Federal and other targeted benefit programs because of their poverty, their disabilities, or their status as veterans. However, many eligible individuals are not currently enrolled. It is imperative that such individuals be identified and receive these benefits as soon as possible.

The extreme poverty of the severely mentally ill population, combined with rising housing costs due to inflation and a growing scarcity of affordable housing, contributes appreciably to housing instability. Among people who can barely meet their rent payments, homelessness is always a threat; almost any unusually large expense, lost job, missed benefit payment, long hospitalization, or theft of cash can make that dreaded prospect a reality.

Efforts to rehabilitate people who are severely mentally ill and homeless should focus on developing their social and work skills to help them become employable (whether in protected or open job markets). Once again, an essential step is to assist these individuals in obtaining all benefits to which they are entitled or for which they are eligible. The extreme poverty of this population, however, and the unlikelihood of finding work in a challenging economic climate also necessitate making more decent, low-cost housing available and providing rent subsidies to make available housing more affordable.

Contact With the Criminal Justice System

People who are homeless—and especially those who also suffer from severe mental illnesses—often come into contact with the criminal justice system, both as offenders and victims. A study in Los Angeles revealed that, compared with other homeless people, those with a mental illness were twice as likely to have been picked up by the police (42 percent vs. 19 percent) during the prior year and more likely to have been victimized on the streets, especially by assault (Farr et al. 1986).

While arrest and incarceration rates are high among the homeless mentally ill population, many of these individuals have been incarcerated for relatively trivial and nonviolent offenses (Dennis and Steadman 1991). Some homeless individuals may engage in illegal activity, such as trespassing, petty theft, shoplifting, and prostitution—crimes of survival that result in arrest. In addition, police often find it easier to incarcerate homeless mentally ill people than to obtain hospitalization or treatment of mental illness. As a result, such individuals are often jailed for minor offenses when their behavior is unacceptably deviant but not necessarily dangerous and never receive the treatment services they desperately need.

Reliance upon the criminal justice system rather than the mental health system to respond to the needs of these individuals perpetuates many of their problems and adds a criminal record to the many barriers already hindering their escape from homelessness. Working relationships among jails, courts, and the treatment system can aid in diverting mentally ill persons to more appropriate and humane alternatives. Training of police and criminal justice staff regarding the characteristics and needs of the severely mentally ill homeless population, and providing better linkages between community mental health programs and the criminal justice system, can help to ensure that these individuals receive appropriate care and planning for their release.

Diminished Social Supports

People who are severely mentally ill and homeless are usually single or divorced and have a very weak system of social support; friends, if any, are few, and family ties are often very tenuous. For example, the homeless severely mentally ill population has been found to have an increased likelihood of a childhood history of foster care, group home placement, or running away from home (Susser et al. 1990).

The withdrawn or alienating behavior of some homeless people with severe mental illnesses may be adaptive in a hostile and dangerous environment, but it may also limit their opportunities to develop supportive relationships. Some people interpret such behavior to mean that these homeless individuals do not want help, although most researchers and experienced street workers agree that it more often reflects fear or a lack of trust rather than a genuine desire to stay homeless. The end result is that many homeless people with severe mental illnesses do not have or cannot use the informal networks that might help them overcome homelessness.

Whenever possible, families should be strengthened and enabled to provide support and housing for their mentally ill relatives. In addition, community and voluntary agencies must provide an ongoing source of assistance and encouragement for individuals with severe mental illness who are homeless and have no natural support systems available.

Minority Status

Racial and ethnic minorities are dramatically overrepresented among homeless populations. For persons of color, homelessness can compound the loss of self and community that is already part of the minority experience. For those who cannot speak English, community living can be particularly difficult. These individuals may have difficulties expressing their needs and communicating with treatment personnel. Multilingual, multicultural outreach workers and treatment staff can be particularly adept at eliciting trust and confidence, especially if they are from the same racial or ethnic background as those they serve.

Like the homeless population in general, minority homeless mentally ill persons have varied needs because of their diversity. Culture and values influence how individuals express problems, how they seek help, and how their problems can best be resolved.

Other Risk Factors

People with a severe mental illness are overrepresented among the homeless population. But since most people with a severe mental illness are not homeless, an important question for prevention efforts is: What factors differentiate those severely mentally ill people who retain housing from those who become homeless? Research findings to date suggest that homelessness is associated with an earlier age of onset of mental illness, co-occurring personality disorders, alcohol and/or other drug abuse disorders and physical illness (e.g., AIDS, tuberculosis), a history of childhood disturbances, violent/aggressive behavior, and housing instability. In brief, among people with severe mental disorders, those at greatest risk of homelessness are both the most severely ill and the most difficult to help.

Photo ©DONNA McADAMS

The Changing Context of Care for Severely Mentally Ill Persons: A Federal Perspective

Background

The organization and delivery of mental health care changed dramatically in the late 1950s and early 1960s. Until then, most severely mentally ill persons were long-term residents of State mental hospitals, where all their care, albeit often inadequate, was administered under one roof. Then, changes in the technology of treating mental disorders (notably the advent of effective psychotherapeutic medications) and in philosophies governing the policies and financing of care for people with mental illnesses permitted and encouraged the gradual shift toward shorter episodes of treatment carried out in a variety of settings outside the mental hospital. The dominance of the State mental hospital as the primary treatment site was challenged as the system gradually became more differentiated, with a variety of care sites developing, many geared toward short-term outpatient care.

As part of the reform effort to improve the care of mentally ill individuals, a policy of *deinstitutionalization* was begun, in which patients were released from the hospitals to community-based care and living situations. A related policy of diversion was also begun, whereby the admission (or readmission) of patients to these hospitals was strongly discouraged. In the mid-1960s, efforts to promote alternatives to hospitalization and encourage new approaches to the care of the mentally ill were powerfully reinforced by Federal legislation. The Community Mental Health Centers Act of 1963 authorized Federal funding for the construction and operation of comprehensive community mental health centers (CMHCs), which provided outpatient, inpatient, emergency, consultation, and partial hospitalization services for all persons living in a defined geographic "catchment" area. As a result of this legislation, 768 CMHCs (approximately half of those initially proposed) were funded in catchment areas across the country. This funding provided the impetus for the proliferation of community-based treatment for mentally ill persons, including those with severe mental illness.

The creation of the Medicaid program in the mid-1960s created fiscal incentives that further promoted a shift in the locus of care from State institutions to community-based treatment programs, notably nursing homes and general hospitals. In addition, the Federal Supplemental Security Income (SSI) Program, and later the Supplemental Security Disability Insurance (SSDI) Program, provided direct entitlements to mentally disabled individuals living

15

in the community. As a result of the confluence of these laws and policies, the State hospital census was reduced nationally from 560,000 in 1955 to 216,000 in 1974; it fell to 100,000 in 1989 (NIMH 1991*b*).

Shifting Responsibilities For Mental Health Services

The changes associated with deinstitutionalization brought with them some long-lasting but often unintended and unanticipated consequences. Among these were the diffusion and blurring of fiscal and administrative responsibilities for the care of people with severe mental illnesses. By 1977, the proliferation of service providers and funders was already so extensive that the U.S. General Accounting Office (1977) had identified fragmentation and lack of coordination among services as prime causes of inadequate care of people with severe mental illnesses.

While funding of the CMHC program fostered a Federal/local partnership in the provision of community mental health care (U.S. Congress 1987), it was not until the late 1970s that the Federal Government initiated efforts to work closely with States. In 1978, NIMH launched the new Community Support Program, which established a focal point for responsibility within each State mental health authority for the coordination of care and treatment for severely mentally ill persons. This effort was important in promoting a working relationship between the Federal Government and States on mental health service delivery issues. The Community Support Program continues to make grants to States to demonstrate and evaluate effective community services to assist severely mentally ill people in meeting their multiple mental health, housing, and support needs. In the Mental Health Systems Act of 1980, Congress noted that, although considerable progress had been made over the decade in making community-based treatment and residential services available, the severely mentally ill population still was not adequately served. It concluded that:

> ... a comprehensive and coordinated array of appropriate private and public mental health and support services for all people in need within specific geographic areas, based upon a cooperative local-State-Federal partnership, remains the most effective and humane way to provide a majority of mentally ill individuals with mental health care and needed support. (U.S. Congress 1980)

In that same year, responding to a recommendation originally made by President Carter's Commission on Mental Health (1978), the Secretary of Health and Human Services commissioned a departmental effort to develop a national plan for the chronically mentally ill (HHS 1980). The resulting report produced a plan that had a number of its most useful recommendations incorporated into public policy (Koyanagi and Goldman 1991). Shortly after the release of this report, Congress passed and President Reagan signed the Alcohol, Drug Abuse, and Mental Health Services (ADMS) Block Grant;

this new legislation signified a growing recognition of the seminal role of States in the provision of mental health services.

Over the years, attempts have been made to make the service system for mentally ill individuals more rational, systematic, and integrated, but the service system remains largely a patchwork of settings, providers, policies, administrative sponsors, and funders. Services for mentally ill individuals are currently delivered through a complex mix of public and private service providers and institutions. These include mental hospitals (State and local, public and private), general hospitals, veterans' hospitals, community mental health centers, residential treatment centers, nursing homes, halfway houses, day treatment centers, board-and-care homes, outpatient clinics, office-based private practitioners (including psychiatrists and other physicians, psychologists, and social workers), psychosocial rehabilitation programs and clubhouses, and self-help groups. However, despite this seeming plethora of care providers, the service system still suffers from severe problems of fragmentation, accessibility, availability, and appropriateness. These problems are particularly acute in the provision of services for severely mentally ill persons who are poor and homeless.

With the enactment of the Stewart B. McKinney Homeless Assistance Act[4] in 1987, the Federal Government recognized the unique service system barriers faced by homeless mentally ill persons. One of the many provisions of the legislation authorized the Mental Health Services for the Homeless Block Grant Program, which was later replaced with the Projects for Assistance in Transition from Homelessness (PATH) Formula Grant Program. The PATH program provides funds to States to develop innovative service interventions specifically targeted to homeless persons with severe mental illness, including those with co-occurring alcohol and/or other drug disorders. The legislation also encourages improved coordination between mental health services and housing.

Mental Health Policies and Homelessness

There are no national data indicating the extent to which deinstitutionalization has contributed directly to homelessness. A substantial proportion of discharged patients—particularly the elderly—were reinstitutionalized; that is, transferred to nursing homes and other long-term-care facilities. Many others were encouraged and helped to live outside the hospital with their families, independently, or in halfway houses, rooming houses, board-and-care homes, single-room-occupancy (SRO) hotels, and other community settings. For some, the relationship between deinstitutionalization and homelessness was indirect: Individuals with appropriate discharge plans became homeless after a relatively long and successful community tenure.

---

[4] Referred to as the McKinney Act.

Some patients were released to communities that lacked sufficient resources to support their basic and specialized needs. Without these necessities, vulnerable people with severe mental illnesses found it difficult to cope with the challenge of locating and retaining housing and the steady income needed to pay for it. When the stock of marginal housing to which they had migrated began to disappear—a casualty of gentrification, demolition, arson, or simple neglect—homelessness frequently became the predictable outcome.

It is important, however, not to overestimate the impact of deinstitutionalization—and severe mental illnesses—on the problem of homelessness at large (see figure 1). Most people with a severe mental illness are not homeless, and most of those who are homeless are not severely mentally ill. Specifically, at any point in time:

- Of the people in the United States with severe mental illnesses—estimated to be as many as 4 million—1/20 are homeless.

- Of the estimated nearly 600,000 homeless people in the United States, 1/3 of the single adults are believed to be severely mentally ill.

It is also important to note that, while the homeless mentally ill population has multiple needs, institutionalization is generally not one of them. In a study, funded jointly by NIMH and the National Institute on Alcohol Abuse and Alcoholism (NIAAA), clinicians recommended inpatient care in a psychiatric setting for 17 percent of the homeless sample evaluated, but long-term hospitalization was recommended for only 1 percent of the sample (Breakey et al. 1989). The authors concluded that "improving the accessibility and availability of community mental health services is more appropriate than advocating reinstitutionalization."

**Figure 1.
The Homeless
and Severely
Mentally Ill
Population**

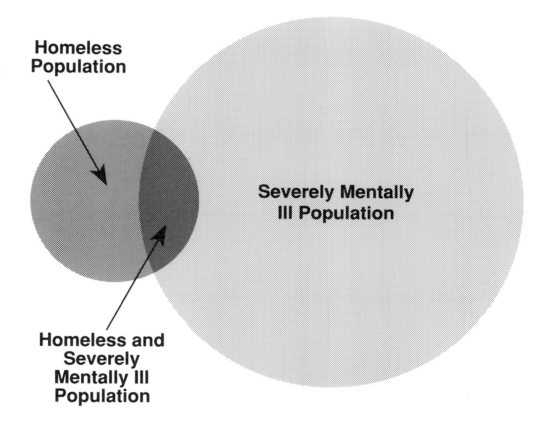

Homeless
Population

Severely Mentally
Ill Population

Homeless and
Severely
Mentally Ill
Population

Photo ©KIM HOPPER

Other Factors Contributing To Homelessness Among Severely Mentally Ill Persons

Homelessness is not a new phenomenon in the United States. But during the late 1970s and 1980s, the familiar, localized populations of transient older men were increasingly joined by new people on the streets: homeless women as well as men, many of them young adults, even families. Many of the new homeless people were African Americans or members of other minority groups, and a substantial proportion appeared to have a severe mental illness in addition to alcoholism and/or other drug abuse problems. Although the data are still sketchy and the baseline is unknown, the U.S. homeless population (as well as the rate of homelessness) appears to have increased steadily during the 1980s, and it still may be growing (Burt 1991). How did this national tragedy happen, and why does it persist? What have been the root causes of homelessness among severely mentally ill people?

Many factors, often intertwined, contribute to the magnitude of the problem of homelessness among the severely mentally ill population. Each of these factors needs to be considered and understood to account for the plight of any given homeless mentally ill individual. The preceding section described the context of changing policies in mental health care and their unintended consequences for severely mentally ill persons. In this section, we describe other broad systemic factors that combine with individual vulnerabilities to result in homelessness.

Lack of Affordable and Appropriate Housing

Among the social and economic factors frequently mentioned as contributing to homelessness in the population at large is the lack of affordable,[5] appropriate housing. Gentrification of urban neighborhoods has virtually eliminated many of the housing options once available to severely mentally ill persons and other indigent populations.

---

[5] The Department of Housing and Urban Development (HUD) defines housing as "affordable" if it costs 30 percent or less of a household's income.

The overall supply of low-cost rental units declined appreciably between the mid-1970s and the mid-1980s—as indicated by the loss of 780,000 units renting under $250 (in constant 1987 dollars) (Interagency Council on the Homeless 1991). Viewed from the perspective of people with very low incomes, the dwindling supply of low-cost housing also meant a dwindling supply of affordablehousing. As overall housing costs rose significantly in the 1980s due to inflation, gentrification, and other factors, Federal housing subsidies rose as well but failed to keep pace with rising costs, leaving many extremely poor individuals either totally unable to meet their escalating rents or devoting an extremely high proportion of their income to rent. In addition, people living on Social Security benefits and other forms of public assistance found that the real value of those benefits was declining in the face of ongoing inflation. Confronted by these numerous economic pressures, many severely mentally ill people—who are among the most vulnerable of the Nation's poor—were unable to compete successfully with other very low-income people for the dwindling stock of affordable housing and became homeless.

Of particular relevance to homelessness among the target population is the declining supply of SRO units in low-cost hotels, which had been a major source of housing for thousands of individuals with severe mental illnesses who lived in the community. Between 1970 and 1982, the Nation lost more than 1 million SRO units as urban renewal and gentrification efforts encouraged their conversion into condominiums and other upscale uses (U.S. Department of Health and Human Services 1984). In New York alone, SRO units declined from 127,000 to 14,000 during that 12-year period (Coalition for the Homeless and SRO Tenants Rights Coalition 1985). Most severely mentally ill people leaving hospitals no longer had the option of living in a SRO unit. Thus, for thousands of severely mentally ill individuals and many other impoverished people living in SROs, the loss of this housing option—for which, usually, no replacement was planned or available—was disastrous and led frequently to homelessness.

To meet the needs of the homeless severely mentally ill population, more low-cost housing of many types needs to be developed or made available. In addition, the accessibility of housing for this population needs to be increased by raising the income of individuals through work and improved access to entitlement and benefit programs and by the use of more housing subsidies to narrow the gap between housing costs and income levels. Furthermore, it is essential to assist those mentally ill individuals who have affordable housing to keep it, whatever the vicissitudes of their life situation.

Fragmentation Of Responsibility And Other Service Integration Problems

People who are severely mentally ill and homeless require an extremely broad array of resources and services—including housing, food, clothing, health and mental health care, treatment of alcohol and other drug abuse, and psychosocial and vocational rehabilitation. Yet in most communities of any size, they must negotiate an extraordinarily complex and disconnected set of bureaucracies to obtain access to these services. Each local agency is usually focused on its particular area of specialized responsibility, making it very difficult to organize and readily provide the breadth of resources required to comprehensively meet the needs of any individual.

In many communities, a homeless person with a severe mental illness may be viewed as a shelter resident by one agency, a mental health client by another, or a substance abuser by a third, with none recognizing and responding to that person's full array of urgent needs. Ironically, the system is structured in a way that makes comprehensive services inaccessible to the very people who need them most. Clearly, special efforts are required to integrate the components flexibly into a coherent constellation of services tailored to meet the unique needs of individuals.

Linking two or more service systems—such as mental health services, housing, and health care—can be difficult, and all too often, in the absence of any real incentives to do so, the attempt is not even made. For example, one critical focal point for prevention efforts should be the transition from institutional care (e.g., release from a general hospital, mental hospital, or jail) to the community. Before severely mentally ill individuals are discharged or released, the reliability and appropriateness of their support resources—including housing—should be assessed and arrangements made for appropriate follow-up care. It is not uncommon for a person to be released without adequate attention to that individual's ability to obtain treatment, housing, or meaningful work or daytime activity in the community. When no alternatives are available, pressures of cost containment in expensive institutional settings complicate discharge planning.

The problems of mounting appropriate service programs for the severely mentally ill homeless population are compounded by the welter of funding mechanisms and agencies involved in their care. Different funding sources, each with its own policies, timetables, and restrictions, contribute to further fragmentation. Public funds—Federal, State, and local—as well as private funds from philanthropic organizations, churches, and individual donors are all part of the funding streams that support services to severely mentally ill homeless people. Many of these sources try (and sometimes succeed) to bring their efforts into better synchrony, but policy differences often inhibit these attempts.

Also of particular importance, given the characteristics of the population, the clinical service system is not well structured to deal with clients who have co-occurring mental illnesses and substance abuse problems (*dually diagnosed persons*). Treatment programs for severe mental illnesses and for alcohol and/or other drug abuse are often administratively, financially, physically, and philosophically separate. Lacking the resources needed to provide the kinds of integrated treatment required for these challenging clients, many programs do not welcome working with homeless people who have co-occurring severe mental illnesses and substance abuse disorders.

In an ideally integrated multi-service system, a homeless person with a severe mental illness should be able to enter by any service "door," be assessed, and obtain access to the full complement of services that individual wants and needs—both immediately and on an ongoing basis. But as services are now structured in most communities, the burden of integration falls on the consumer, not the system. Many of those consumers, lacking the supportive services they need to sustain their best level of functioning, become far more ill and dysfunctional than their clinical disorder per se warrants.

Community Resistance and Discrimination

Communities, both large and small, have been attempting to find ways to end homelessness. Despite many heartening achievements, most are encountering obstacles that make an inherently complex task unnecessarily difficult. Among these obstacles are resistance and opposition from neighbors within the same communities.

People with severe mental illnesses have a long history of being stigmatized—reviled, shunned, shut away, and in previous eras, killed. Before the advent of effective medications and psychosocial treatments, communities often found the behavior of such people too bizarre and unpredictable to tolerate in their midst. Now it is possible for most people with severe mental illnesses to live and work productively and comfortably in communities if certain conditions are fulfilled: (1) they receive ongoing treatment and other support services to remain functioning well; (2) their needs for housing, income, and other basic necessities are met; and (3) residents of neighborhoods are educated to understand the nature of mental illnesses and the people they affect, as well as the requirements of civil rights laws that prohibit discrimination against people with mental disabilities.

Unfortunately, some homeless individuals with a severe mental illness resemble the classical stereotypes of mentally ill people because they, like generations before them, are receiving no treatment or care. Their behavior is indeed strange—especially when exacerbated by substance abuse—and many community members are understandably discomforted by their presence on the streets. That discomfort also extends to the prospect of permitting such people to live in residential neighborhoods. Both formal and informal measures are often used to thwart the local placement of housing for homeless mentally ill individuals. As a result, the "not-in-my-back-yard" (NIMBY) syndrome constitutes a major barrier to the development and location of housing for this population.

The report of the Advisory Commission on Regulatory Barriers to Affordable Housing (1991) recommends that all local governments initiate a strategy of removing barriers to creating special housing for people with disabilities. The strategy should include a comprehensive and systematic review of zoning, subdivision ordinances, building codes, and related development-control ordinances and administrative procedures to identify excessive barriers to housing affordability and opportunity.

Legal protections are available—but underutilized—to help the homeless severely mentally ill population gain access to public and private housing and other services in the community. Three Federal statutes—Section 504 of the Rehabilitation Act of 1973, the Fair Housing Amendments Act of 1988 (FHAA), and the more recently enacted Americans with Disabilities Act of 1990 (ADA)—prohibit discrimination against individuals with mental disabilities. However, the definition of disability in these laws excludes current users of illegal drugs, an exclusion that poses problems for some dually diagnosed homeless individuals.

Section 504 prohibits discrimination in any federally funded program, including housing projects, employment, transportation, and education. The FHAA, which expanded the coverage of Title VIII of the Civil Rights Act of 1968 to include individuals with handicaps as a protected class, applies to all public or private housing, whether or not it is federally funded. In addition, the FHAA makes illegal any zoning regulations that improperly limit housing opportunities for people with disabilities. The ADA prohibits discrimination in private employment; by State and local governments in all programs and services; and in goods, services, or accommodations available in 12 types of public accommodation. Problematic land-use rules include those that differentiate between housing for handicapped and nonhandicapped people without well-founded nondiscriminatory reasons, and those that fail to reasonably accommodate housing for handicapped people. The adequacy of these protections remains to be tested through the development of case law. Increased public awareness of these provisions is necessary to reduce the effect of discrimination on access to appropriate housing.

As the NIMBY phenomenon suggests, the misunderstanding and stigmatization of people with a severe mental illness (and sometimes people with any mental illness) may extend beyond attitudes and behavior toward single individuals to shape the nature of public policies and priorities regarding the mentally ill population at large. There is ample evidence, for example, that in public funding for clinical care, as in third-party coverage for health insurance, mental illnesses are shortchanged relative to other illnesses (Judd 1990). The same appears to be true of public funding for services for the severely mentally ill homeless population.

More public education and dissemination of information about severe mental illnesses and homelessness are needed to aid public understanding, reduce stigmatization, and strengthen advocacy efforts for this population. In addition, stronger enforcement of relevant anti-discrimination legislation is needed.

Inadequate Focus on Prevention

The condition of homelessness for any given individual is dynamic and fluid. The absolute size of the homeless mentally ill population does not accurately reflect the numbers of individuals who move in and out of the condition of homelessness over a period of time. The Task Force believes that it is as necessary to prevent entry into homelessness as it is to help those individuals who are already homeless. Prevention efforts are not only humane but can also be cost-effective in the long run.

One approach to preventing homelessness among hospitalized mentally ill persons is appropriate discharge planning from State hospitals and other inpatient facilities, as well as careful planning for release from jails and shelters. Research has demonstrated that for psychiatric inpatients, the greatest risk of homelessness occurred immediately following hospital discharge (Newman 1991). Therefore, effective discharge planning requires linkages between hospitals and community-based programs to ensure the availability and coordination of housing and supportive services.

Two provisions of the SSI program, in particular, can make a significant difference in people's lives as they undergo the difficult transition back to the community. A pre-release program currently exists for potential SSI recipients whose release from an institution is imminent; these individuals can apply for benefits 30 days prior to discharge and receive benefit payments when they re-enter the community. SSI provisions also allow payments (based on the full benefit rate) for individuals who are temporarily (for up to 3 months) in medical or psychiatric facilities and need to maintain a living arrangement to which they can return. Communities also need to have the capacity to respond to both psychiatric and housing crises on a timely basis to prevent more serious problems before they occur.

Since many severely mentally ill persons are at considerable risk of homelessness, prevention efforts should also focus on preventing eviction or unnecessary loss of housing for other reasons. These efforts should include assisting individuals in obtaining benefits for which they are eligible, locating and securing affordable housing options, providing necessary treatment and supportive services to those individuals residing in the community, and educating these individuals concerning their rights and responsibilities in tenant-landlord relationships. Some researchers have suggested that intensive support immediately after placement in housing is particularly critical to ensure residential tenure (Notkin et al. 1990).

Resource Limitations

During the past decade, a body of knowledge and experience has been growing about effective ways to deliver community-based services to people with severe mental illnesses, including those who are homeless. Concurrently, advances in clinical research have refined and improved techniques for diagnosing, treating, and rehabilitating these individuals. At the same time, essential resources—Federal, State, and local, public and private—have been devoted to providing services needed by the homeless population, including the mentally ill subgroups.

At the Federal level, for example, all the Federal agencies with representation on our Task Force—e.g., the Department of Housing and Urban Development (HUD), the Department of Health and Human Services (HHS), the Department of Veterans Affairs (VA), the Department of Labor (DOL), the Department of Education (DOEd), and the Department of Justice (DOJ)—offer important resources and mainstream programs for target groups (such as low-income or disabled individuals) that may include homeless and/or mentally ill individuals.[6] Other programs are targeted to the severely mentally ill population or to many homeless individuals. A small number of programs are specifically targeted to individuals who are severely mentally ill and homeless or at risk of homelessness.

However, many community programs for severely mentally ill homeless people do not reflect the current state of the art in service delivery and do not always take best advantage of essential resources that could directly benefit their clientele. Given the important role of the Federal Government in providing resources relevant to the home-

---

[6] For detailed information on these Federal programs, readers are referred to *The 1990 Annual Report of the Interagency Council on the Homeless*. The 1991 edition will be available later this year.

less severely mentally ill population, it is essential that the relevant Federal agencies provide technical assistance to States and communities that will improve access to these programs. In addition, the Federal Government should enhance its role in disseminating research results that would aid in designing more effective service systems for the homeless severely mentally ill population. While an expansion of resources for aiding this population could be put to good use, we must also make far better use of the resources we have.

At present, some financial incentives in the service system are, in fact, disincentives or have other unintended effects that are counterproductive. Current reimbursement mechanisms do not cover the full range of necessary services and do not encourage alternatives to hospitalization. Furthermore, they encourage dependence on an already burdened public system. For example, anecdotal reports suggest that the reduced Medicaid limits on acute care in general hospitals may create financial pressures on hospitals that result in increasing referrals to State mental hospitals. Lacking any persuasive evidence or incentives for change, third-party payers often resist improving reimbursement mechanisms for mental health care. Stereotypes about the nature of severe mental illnesses and the stigma they engender account for some of the unrealistic limitations on reimbursement. But simple lack of data plays a role as well.

Relationships between the costs and benefits of different treatments for mental illnesses are largely unknown. Policymakers fear that the enormous latent demand for services will bankrupt any program that provides full benefits—a fear that seems to be based on current service structures and reimbursement guidelines. However, this fear may be unfounded. Providing effective integrated services may well be cost-effective. A thorough analysis of alternatives to existing and proposed reimbursement options is essential to clarify the budgetary implications of changes in benefits.

Efforts to end homelessness among people with severe mental illnesses require many types of resources. However, because the current national economy necessitates extreme fiscal restraint in the expenditure of public and private funds, citizens and legislators face very difficult choices. In the competition for scarce resources during such periods, certain fragile and stigmatized populations who for the most part cannot advocate effectively for themselves may fare badly unless others advocate intensively on their behalf.

The front pages of today's newspapers bring us daily reminders of the fact that, although the plight of homeless severely mentally ill people is a national scandal, deep cuts are being made in budgets for human services, many of which are essential to the rehabilitation of these poor and severely disabled Americans. Although the voluntary sector plays an essential role in providing fundamental resources for the homeless population, it cannot be expected to provide or fund the extensive network of professional services required to meet the needs of this population. Public sources of funding will be needed to support service programs targeted specifically to homeless severely mentally ill people as well as more generic mainstream programs upon which this population—like so many others of the Nation's poor—depends.

Photo ©KIM HOPPER

Toward a National Strategy To End Homelessness Among People With Severe Mental Illnesses

Introduction

The findings presented on the preceding pages describe a poignant dilemma facing our Nation. Nearly 200,000 of our most vulnerable and disabled citizens are homeless and mentally ill, seemingly ignored by a society indifferent to their plight. Most lack:

- permanent, safe, decent housing;

- a source of income or employment;

- treatment to provide relief from the disturbing symptoms of severe mental illnesses (and possibly substance abuse);

- basic health care; and

- any social support network.

At the same time, a growing number of concerned and caring citizens, working through both public and private auspices, are struggling to provide essential resources to homeless severely mentally ill people in their community, their State, and their Nation. However, the funds, programs, organizations, efforts, and goodwill now devoted to improving the lives of homeless people with severe mental illnesses fall far short of their intended effect.

On the pages to follow, we present a course of action—and the principles guiding it—that can help our Nation complete the task at hand: putting an end to homelessness among severely mentally ill Americans. We build upon the knowledge, experience, and resources that communities around the country already have in place. We stress an approach that encourages the integration of an extremely broad array of flexible services and service resources.

Both the nature of the population and the social context lead to this emphasis. In the first instance, disability and deprivation combine in the homeless severely mentally ill population to make virtually every aspect of life problematic. Many severely mentally ill individuals cannot maneuver the fragmented, disconnected systems of care we now have. A service system for such individuals must be integrated and comprehensive in structure and orientation to address their multiple needs, while ensuring appropriate accountability. In the second instance, many essential components of an appropriate service system for homeless people with a severe mental illness are already in place, but disjointed. Components of a system of care for these people must be integrated to allow for access to all elements of care regardless of an individual's first point of contact with the system. It is both humane and, we believe, economical to enhance the system's efficiency on behalf of these individuals.

Principles

More than a decade has been devoted to developing and assessing services for homeless people who have severe mental illnesses. The combination of practical experience and research has provided an increasingly solid foundation of knowledge about the needs of this population and effective ways to address them. The following principles, drawn from this knowledge base, should serve as the cornerstone for all aspects of service delivery to this population.

Access, Empowerment, and Responsibility

- Homelessness is an unacceptable life condition for anyone, but particularly for individuals with severe mental illnesses. Decent, affordable, and stable housing, coupled with appropriate treatment and supports when necessary, should be accessible to all such individuals.

- Homeless mentally ill individuals should be assisted to access and use the mainstream (housing, income support, and mental health) services and resources for which they are eligible.

- The dignity of homeless mentally ill individuals must be respected. To the fullest extent feasible, they, like all other members of society, should be educated and empowered to make choices in matters affecting their lives and to accept responsibility for those choices.

Diversity and Flexibility

- Homeless mentally ill individuals differ appreciably in their racial, cultural, and ethnic backgrounds. These differences can significantly affect outreach, treatment, and rehabilitation needs. Staff should reflect the racial/ethnic makeup of their client populations, and must be fluent in the language(s) of those they serve.

- Homeless mentally ill individuals also have differing preferences, treatment histories, strengths, and motivations—to say nothing of their heterogeneity in gender, age, illness, and disability. Recognition of these differences and sensitivity in responding to them are essential prerequisites for any program intended to serve this population.

- In responding to this diversity, a system of care for homeless mentally ill people needs to be comprehensive in the services it provides, but all individuals do not necessarily need all service elements. A system also should be able to respond flexibly to the varied and changing needs of individuals over time and should offer a range of alternatives.

Peer, Family, and Other Natural Supports

- Services should ultimately be offered in the least restrictive and most normal setting, one that builds upon community resources and peer supports.

- Consumers, families, and community members must be involved in ongoing efforts to plan, deliver, monitor, and evaluate the quality of care.

- Families can be important sources of support and sustenance in the care of individuals with severe mental illnesses and in the prevention of homelessness. Efforts should be made to provide resources that enhance families' supportive roles and, when consistent with the individual's choice, to reconnect homeless mentally ill individuals with their families.

Local, State, and Federal Participation

- Local determination: Because the values, needs, and resources of communities vary greatly, services need to be locally driven and reflect the particular local environment.

- State coordination: State government should play an important role in working with localities to design and implement comprehensive systems of treatment, housing, and supportive services, and to set standards.

- Federal leadership: The Federal Government should provide strong leadership, as well as financial incentives, that will encourage the development of better systems of care for homeless mentally ill individuals.

The Goal: An Integrated Service System for Homeless People With Severe Mental Illnesses

Introduction: The Vision of Systems Integration

Attempts to help homeless people with severe mental illnesses rebuild their lives need to address and improve all aspects of their life situation. Improving services for them requires the creation of a system of care addressed to the whole person. Thus, there is growing consensus that an array of basic life supports (e.g., food, clothing, and shelter) and specialized services is required to respond adequately to the needs of this extremely disadvantaged population. The American Psychiatric Association's Task Force on the Homeless Mentally Ill succinctly described the ideal service system as "... a comprehensive and integrated system of care with designated responsibility, with accountability, and with adequate fiscal resources" (Lamb 1984).

Any successful strategy would have to include integration at the client level (such as case management models), the local level (such as the creation of public mental health authorities and service coalitions, managed care, and "one-stop-shopping" models), and the State level (such as coordination of housing and human service planning and financing, and application and use of special waiver authorities) as well as the Federal level (such as the Task Force on Homelessness and Severe Mental Illness). Such integration can be facilitated by a common data system that links clients to services, and diverse services and resources to each other. Services integration will also require the creative use of mainstream and targeted Federal resources and State, local, and private funds relevant to the needs of homeless mentally ill persons.

No matter how many agencies or individual providers are involved, one will need to be identified as the lead authority at each level of government, accountable for ensuring access, appropriateness, and continuity of services. Moreover, people who are homeless and severely mentally ill require a system of care that they can maneuver, one that is capable of a coherent response to their many needs. Integrating administrative, fiscal, and clinical authority is one of the most problematic service system issues related to the homeless severely mentally ill population. Previous efforts to promote services integration for the severely mentally ill population (e.g., NIMH Community Support Program and the Robert Wood Johnson Foundation's Program on Mental Illness) can provide valuable lessons, however. In addition, there are many emerging models that integrate one or more of the specialized services that the homeless mentally ill population requires (e.g., the integration of mental health and substance abuse treatment).

In summary, there is a growing knowledge base of research and experience that can be used by States and communities in designing strategies for systems integration. The ultimate form by which this integration is achieved will need to reflect local needs, resources, and priorities.

Essential Service System Components

The Task Force found widespread agreement about the essential elements of an integrated service system for the homeless mentally ill population (see figure 2). Based upon the extensive contributions of our Advisory Committee as well as commissioned papers, research reviews, and advice and testimony from many ad hoc groups and individual informants, the key components of such a system have been identified as follows.

Assertive Outreach

Most severely mentally ill people who are homeless find it difficult, if not impossible, to improve their lives appreciably on their own. Disorientation, mistrust, fear of rehospitalization, ignorance, lack of motivation, language problems, and poverty keep such people from enlisting the aid of other

**Figure 2.
Elements of
An Integrated
System of Care
to End
Homelessness
Among
Severely
Mentally Ill
Persons**

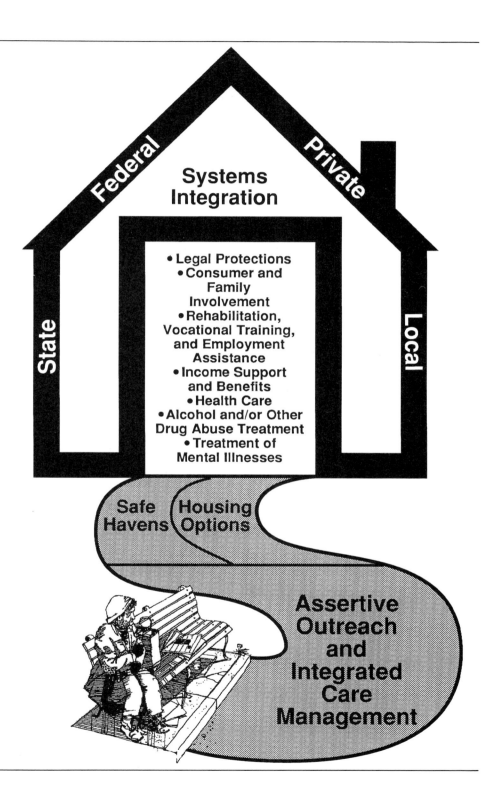

Systems
Integration

Federal

Private

State

Local

• Legal Protections
• Consumer and
Family
Involvement
• Rehabilitation,
Vocational Training,
and Employment
Assistance
• Income Support
and Benefits
• Health Care
• Alcohol and/or Other
Drug Abuse Treatment
• Treatment of
Mental Illnesses

Safe
Havens

Housing
Options

Assertive
Outreach
and
Integrated
Care
Management

people and maintaining contact with many of the resources that might significantly enhance their well-being. In addition, many homeless mentally ill people are unwilling and/or unable to accommodate to the conventions of traditional service systems, such as keeping appointments for office visits (which also requires accessible transportation).

Service providers, therefore, must meet homeless individuals on their own terms and on their own turf. These vital workers must address immediate survival needs (such as food, clothing, and shelter) and provide or connect these individuals with sustained treatment and support, based on ongoing assessment of their clinical conditions and needs. The process of engaging homeless people is time-consuming, protracted, and staff-intensive. But by offering patient, persistent, and continuing contacts over relatively long periods of time, outreach workers can establish the trusting relationships that are essential to engage and help mentally ill people living on the streets. Outreach strategies can also be used to help people in shelters move into more stable housing situations that are linked with supportive services.

In general, outreach teams are likely to be most effective if they can offer services valued by homeless people with severe mental illnesses. Outreach in the absence of attractive options for these people is pointless. For example, one study demonstrated that it was difficult to get homeless people who were located in airports to consider alternative living sites when the provider could offer nothing better than what they already had (Hopper 1991). Compared to the airport, the shelters were more degrading, unsanitary, crowded, and unsafe.

Outreach workers and service providers should be selected or trained to be fluent in and sensitive to the language and culture of those they serve. Of course, they should be trained to recognize clinical syndromes, their symptoms, and their implications. Given the special needs of the population served, outreach services need to be conducted with low client/staff ratios and great flexibility. Staffing for outreach efforts can be enhanced by using consumers, whose own experiences with being mentally ill and homeless can be invaluable in locating potential clients and gaining their trust.

Street outreach must include the capacity for an emergency response as well as engagement. Homeless mentally ill individuals often are found living in life-threatening circumstances and/or in precarious locations. For example, the New York City Transit Police estimate that 5,000 people lived in the bowels of the city's subway system in 1989, many of them persons with severe mental illnesses. That year alone, 79 individuals were either electrocuted or hit by trains (Rabasca 1992). Similarly, some homeless mentally ill individuals living on the streets are unable or unwilling to go indoors in below-freezing temperatures. For reasons such as these, crisis outreach teams need to be available to evaluate individuals and transport them, if necessary, to emergency or inpatient services. Backup medical and psychiatric support is essential to ensure access to involuntary treatment when it is needed.

Drop-in centers, which are generally small, accessible, store-front locations, are often effective in engaging portions of the homeless mentally ill population that are typically not reached by other service interventions (Levine 1984). Distinguished from more formal programs by their casual accessibility, these centers can offer a place to sit during the day, a place to sleep at night, or both. They are particularly inviting to many homeless mentally ill individuals because they ask few questions and make no demands. Like other outreach efforts, they often become a bridge to the more formal service delivery and/or shelter network.

Although assistance with survival needs is a crucial aspect of outreach, high priority must also be given to shifting the locus of service as soon as possible from street sites to residential settings. Therefore, outreach teams need to link homeless mentally ill people with safe havens and other readily accessible and secure reception places as soon as it is practicable (see Safe Havens below).

Integrated Care Management

Another essential service system component for people who are homeless and severely mentally ill is known as *case management* or *integrated care management*. (The latter term refers to an evolving form of case management that builds on the research and practical experience of case management models designed to provide services to homeless mentally ill individuals.) The goals of integrated care management are common to many case management models: enhancing continuity of care, access to services, and efficiency and accountability of service provision and integration. Essentially, there must be a sustained relationship with someone who knows each client as an individual, and who understands the client's needs and how to address them.

In addition, an integrated care manager helps the client to negotiate continuously the maze of disparate Federal, State, and local services. This individual, often a member of a multidisciplinary team, can help clients in obtaining benefits and entitlements; assist with and arrange access to health and dental care, housing, and transportation; coordinate appointments and monitor compliance with mental health and substance abuse treatments; and see that the client receives timely, appropriate services. Care management may also include assessing the need for a *representative payee*—a responsible person selected to manage disability and welfare incomes for clients deemed incapable of doing so.

Given the complexity, multiplicity, and urgency of the needs of homeless people with severe mental illnesses, integrated care management must be extremely flexible, with all dimensions of service delivery suitably adapted.

That is, the duration of integrated care management is indefinite, the frequency of contact is high, the caseloads are low, the focus and siting of services are extremely broad and flexible, and the availability of services is continuous. In addition, to the extent possible, the authority for clinical and administrative decisions resides with the integrated care management team, and decisions are negotiated directly with homeless mentally ill persons. To accomplish integrated care management, all caregivers who work with the homeless severely mentally ill population must be trained to use all necessary community resources and work together toward common goals. Meeting these comprehensive objectives requires incentives for staff recruitment as well as ongoing training, support, and supervision.

Effective integrated care management can improve the overall functioning of homeless people with severe mental illnesses, reduce their contact with police and with crisis and inpatient services, and stimulate closer involvement with families and housing providers. By establishing a continuing relationship and by encouraging and facilitating more appropriate use of community-based services, this form of integrated care management may also lessen the "revolving door" of rehospitalization and homelessness.

For some homeless individuals, integrated care management may need to continue well after housing has been\obtained. If integrated care managers (and funds) were assigned to clients, not to institutions, a care manager could work with a given client over time throughout all of the client's contacts with the system—whether at a shelter, in a hospital, or in a jail.

Safe Havens

For many mentally ill people who have been living on the streets, the transition to stable housing is best made in stages, starting with a small, highly supportive environment where an individual can feel at ease and out of danger and is subject to relatively few demands. Most communities offer shelters as a first point of refuge for all homeless people. But these settings are often not well suited to people with severe mental illnesses, and vice versa. Some shelters will not admit people who are psychotic and unwilling to accept treatment immediately; others exclude people who use alcohol or other drugs. From the perspective of severely mentally ill people who are accepted in large public shelters, these facilities are often frightening places—crowded sites that offer no safety, peace, or privacy, where assault and theft are common, and these vulnerable individuals are all too often the victims. It is essential to address the most basic needs of these individuals in a humane and comprehensive way, not merely to place homeless people out of sight.

A respite from street life is necessary to achieve relative stability and to permit professional staff to adequately assess clients' long-term needs and prospects. The skills needed for survival on the streets (such as the need to mistrust strangers and use hostility as a defense) differ greatly from those needed for accommodation indoors. Before they are ready and able to adhere to rules and program requirements, many people with severe mental illnesses need not only shelter from the harshness of street living, but time to reflect and learn to trust helpers.

Hence, there is a need to expand the array of appropriately staffed, low-demand environments that will provide a safe, sanitary residence for homeless people with severe mental illnesses, support and assist them in overcoming specific problems that impede access to permanent housing, and develop the integrated supports needed for successful residential tenure. One type of facility that has been proposed, known as a *safe haven*, could offer an attractive portal of entry to the service system for such individuals. It is a small facility (for fewer than 25 people) that offers semiprivate accommodations and basic services (such as food, showers, clothing, and shelter) as well as other necessities, such as telephones, a mailing address, and a place to lock up and store belongings.

Safe havens can accommodate homeless mentally ill persons coming from shelters or emergency rooms (when hospitalization is not required) as well as those coming directly from the street. They offer a relatively stable and secure environment for people not yet ready to participate in more mainstream housing options—both temporary and permanent—for homeless individuals. Unlike some shelters, safe havens offer consistency of the same bed each night, and belongings are safe. Residents are not required to vacate the premises during the day, and they may stay as long as they wish. (Such arrangements can facilitate the treatment of physical illnesses, which often require bed rest and complex medication regimens.)

Staff/client ratios in these facilities need to be sufficiently high to ensure safety and security and to assess needs, plan treatment, and link individuals to entitlements and services. Staff of safe havens should reflect the ethnic, cultural, and language background of clients being served. In addition, staff members should be familiar with community resources for treatment of physical and mental illnesses and for housing and social supports. To build a sense of empowerment and a supportive sense of community, safe haven staff should encourage (but not require) residents to participate in the operation of the facility.

Housing

> No combination of mental health, social services, case management, health care, or advocacy will be effective in meeting the needs of homeless mentally ill persons in the absence of the availability of affordable housing. (Chicago Coalition for the Homeless 1991)

Like other homeless people, those who are severely mentally ill need housing arrangements that are safe, clean, appropriate, and affordable. Given the extreme poverty of the population, housing must be made affordable through housing subsidies, greater access to entitlements and benefits, and increased employment opportunities. The long-term goal should be to obtain permanent housing, linked and readily accessible to community-based services, for each homeless severely mentally ill person. Given the heterogeneity of the homeless mentally ill population, an array of housing options should be available to meet individual preferences, rehabilitative needs, and abilities. Although the physical structure of housing for the severely mentally ill population need be no different than housing for any other population, such housing might include, when necessary, supervision to assist individuals in their transition back to the community.

Housing for the target population is generally derived from two essential sources: the open market of current housing and the development of new housing through conversion, renovation, and new construction. Although an adequate stock of housing is available in most parts of the country, there is often a shortage of affordable housing for people with very low incomes, such as homeless severely mentally ill persons. Thus, considerable creativity and flexibility are required to develop and finance housing affordable to this population. Given the complexities of housing development, mental health providers need to use housing experts to help them in this process. Special needs housing development, like other low-cost housing development, requires incentives. For example, some organizations are helping nonprofits develop affordable special needs units through tax credits.

Federal and State housing policies designed to assist the homeless mentally ill population must be flexible to meet the circumstances of individual localities. Local housing stock, availability of mental health and support services, and the concentration, characteristics, and needs of homeless mentally ill people vary from location to location, thus requiring policies and programs that are adaptable to local conditions. For instance, the nature of housing resources will probably differ in urban and rural settings. Additionally, the needs of different segments of the homeless mentally ill population (e.g., singles vs. single parents, young vs. elderly, women vs. men) can be expected to have a bearing on the design and operation of housing programs. Attention should be paid to the number of homeless mentally ill people who are placed in any one housing arrangement; where possible, housing should be integrated and include a mix of populations (e.g., people with and without severe mental illnesses). Finally, housing should be located to provide easy access to public transportation.

While it is essential to acknowledge the important role of emergency shelters in "housing" homeless people with severe mental illnesses, we agree with the warning articulated by the Institute of Medicine's Committee on Health Care for Homeless People:

> Shelters should not become a permanent network of new institutions or substandard human service organizations. As desirable housing is developed, the shelter system should be substantially reduced in

size and returned to its original intent to provide short-term crisis intervention. (Institute of Medicine 1988)

The spectrum of housing provided to homeless mentally ill individuals should include low-demand, transitional, long-term, crisis, and respite settings, with an appropriate variety of support services available. These residential settings might be provided through a variety of housing models including safe havens, emergency shelters, group homes, half-way houses, foster homes, board-and-care homes, nursing homes, clustered and scattered-site apartments, SROs, condominiums, and houses.

Stable housing should be the goal of any housing effort. It must be recognized, however, that homeless people who suffer from a severe mental illness may not always move along a housing continuum beginning in a low-demand emergency shelter and ending in an independent scattered-site apartment. Rather, these individuals may need different kinds of housing, structure, supervision, and supportive service arrangements at various points in their lives. In addition, mechanisms need to be in place to ensure that housing is retained during periods of hospitalization.

For homeless people with a severe mental illness and co-occurring substance abuse problems, special housing considerations include the need to develop *wet* houses (where on-site alcohol is tolerated), *damp* houses (where off-site substance use is tolerated), and *dry* houses (where abstinence is a prerequisite for tenancy). Abstinence may be the goal of treatment, but homeless people with co-occurring mental health and substance abuse problems will require some form of housing or shelter until that goal is achieved.

While housing is essential, it is not sufficient to meet the needs of the homeless mentally ill population. The coordinated provision of housing and services (at Federal, State, and local levels) is crucial to maintaining many homeless mentally ill people in housing. To ensure the well-being and safety of severely mentally ill tenants and other community members, it is important that such tenants (and their landlords) have available to them a wide range of flexible supportive services such as mobile crisis-intervention that can provide mental health consultation and access to emergency psychiatric evaluations, backed up by accessible resources for emergency psychiatric treatment. The challenges of linking housing with supportive services are often particularly formidable in rural communities where large geographic distances and transportation problems must be considered.

Because there is generally a paucity of information and research on the housing needs and housing outcomes of homeless mentally ill persons, it is imperative that mental health and housing providers, consumers, and researchers focus attention on these critical issues. The development of such an information base by the mental health community would help inform housing planners, developers, and communities about housing needs for this target population; additionally, it would assist consumers, providers, and families in choosing the most appropriate setting available.

Coordinating housing and services generally requires an active collaboration or partnership between housing and mental health providers. The role of the mental health service provider is to assess the tenant's readiness to assume more independent living, to arrange for and ensure implementation of any necessary treatment or supports, to be available in case of an emergency or special needs, and, more broadly, to identify and advocate for the housing needs of mentally ill individuals.

Cooperative agreements between housing providers and service providers have been used as a mechanism for identifying responsibility and accountability. In 1986, the Robert Wood Johnson Foundation selected nine cities to participate in a 5-year program to develop community-wide systems of care for people with severe mental illnesses. In addition to integrating administrative, fiscal, and clinical responsibility for the severely mentally ill population, housing integration was promoted through the contribution of Section 8 housing certificates to the program participants by HUD. (The certificates guarantee a rent subsidy for private housing for very low-income individuals certified as eligible by a public housing agency.) A major element in the success of this program was the establishment of special housing development corporations to coordinate housing and services at the community level. While these projects were not specifically focused on homeless populations, their potential for generating knowledge on systems integration is significant.

In some systems of care, it may be helpful to have housing assistance coordinators or integrated care managers help clients find apartments and negotiate leases. Frequently, the symptoms of severe mental illnesses impede individuals' abilities to find vacancies, negotiate complex bureaucracies, and convince landlords of their desirability as tenants. To assist clients and their helpers in identifying prospective housing, one city government has funded a computer-based model that links severely mentally ill homeless individuals with housing vacancies. The computer program surveys all residential facilities available to homeless mentally ill individuals in the city and identifies potential housing sources, including shelters and community-based programs. Tracking available vacancies in new and existing supportive housing accommodations and matching prospective residents' characteristics and preferences with available vacancies are primary functions of this service.

Private landlords are far more likely to rent to a homeless person with severe mental illnesses if they have met the care manager, have the program's assurance that rent will be paid, and know there is someone they can call in a crisis. When people with a severe mental illness are given appropriate supportive services, they usually make excellent tenants.

Treatment of Mental Illnesses

Most homeless people with severe mental illnesses can be treated effectively in the community on an outpatient basis. However, because severe mental disorders tend to be long-lasting or recurrent, people with these disorders need ongoing treatment to lessen the symptoms, impairments, and disruptions they produce. For a variety of reasons—including active avoidance of traditional treatments by some individuals as well as resistance by some caregivers to dealing with certain difficult clients—the treatment needs of the homeless mentally ill population are largely unmet. In addition, unlike shelter, food, and other fundamental necessities offered to these persons, treatment of mental illness is not often high on their list of priorities. Thus it has been suggested that treatment of mental illnesses be "bundled" with (but not a prerequisite for) other basic services that address immediate needs for daily living.

Many homeless individuals—particularly those who were once long-term residents of mental hospitals—have had quite negative experiences with the mental health system. Too often, the label of "treatment resistant" is used to justify gaps in the service system or to rationalize an individual's descent into homelessness. The Task Force agrees with a prominent community health psychiatrist, who was quoted as saying:

> If you define treatment resistant as unwilling to accept any kind of help, then it is simply not true [that homeless severely mentally ill people are treatment resistant]. If you say they are unwilling to accept traditional approaches—such as showing up at an office for an appointment—clearly they are treatment resistant. Then we are left with two options. We can decide that the traditional approach is all we have to offer, or we can come up with something they will find acceptable. (Stein in Moran 1992)

Some younger homeless individuals with severe mental illnesses have never had mental health or substance abuse treatment of any type and are unaware that it might help them function better. In many rural areas, there is a paucity of trained mental health professionals available to provide services to severely mentally ill persons. Given the varied experiences, expectations, illnesses, treatment histories, and needs of homeless mentally ill people, it is essential that they be assessed carefully and encouraged to understand the nature of their illness and the specific therapeutic approaches—whether biological, psychosocial, or both—most appropriate to treat it.

In general, this population requires access to the full range of treatment and rehabilitative services a community should offer, including needs assessment, diagnosis and treatment planning, medication management, counseling and supportive therapy, hospitalization and inpatient care, 24-hour crisis-response services (e.g., backup to landlords), and habilitation and social skills training. In addition, special efforts are needed to integrate

43

mental health and substance abuse treatment for people who require both (see Alcohol and/or Other Drug Abuse Treatment below) and to improve hospital discharge planning policies to ensure that appropriate housing, mental health care, and support services are available in the community following hospitalization.

Planning appropriate treatment and support services for a homeless person with a severe mental illness requires a careful diagnostic work-up and an ongoing assessment of the person's mastery of basic life skills, i.e., those that are necessary to meet personal and social needs. Individualized treatment planning—including, for some people, the need for sophisticated psychopharmacologic treatment—should be developed with the homeless mentally ill person's participation. Complications or medication side effects should be anticipated, and problem-solving should occur ahead of time rather than during crises. Compliance with treatment plans must be monitored and supported, an important function of the designated care manager. Given the complex life situations of people who have experienced or are experiencing the trauma of homelessness, assessment and planning require time and regular reevaluation.

Ideally, hospitals should be used only when treatment goals cannot be achieved elsewhere. At times, brief periods (usually 2 to 3 weeks) of hospitalization may be useful to assess individuals' illnesses and provide treatment to help them gain control of symptoms. Access to voluntary hospital beds for homeless severely mentally ill individuals is extremely limited in some communities, however. This is a serious concern because, in the case of extreme disorders of thinking or mood, hospital treatment may be required either on a voluntary basis or an involuntary basis, when individuals are found to be dangerous to themselves or others. In general, commitment—be it inpatient or outpatient—should be of an individual to a system of care rather than to any single institution or provider.

Discharge planning should begin at the time a person is admitted to a hospital. The period immediately preceding the discharge of a person with a severe mental illness from a hospital represents one opportunity to prevent homelessness and encourage continuing treatment and rehabilitation. Each person requires a treatment and rehabilitation plan in order to minimize the amount of time spent in such settings and maximize his or her long-term housing stability.

Alcohol and/or Other Drug Abuse Treatment

The lives of at least half of the homeless severely mentally ill population are further complicated by alcohol and other drug abuse (NIMH 1991a). Such dually diagnosed individuals require skilled assessment and a combination of mental health and substance abuse interventions. The latter should include access to detoxification, treatment, and recovery services (e.g., referral and self-help services). Residential services are also required that include wet, damp, and dry housing—e.g., small residential settings geared specifically to people at various stages in the recovery process (NIAAA 1992).

People with dual diagnoses present a complex clinical picture, and the separation, or at best the fragmentation, of mental health and substance abuse services in many States increases their difficulty in accessing the services most likely to help them. Traditional alcohol and other drug abuse treatment programs, like traditional treatments for mental illnesses, have been shown to have limited efficacy for this population. However, promising integrative approaches are being implemented and tested (NIAAA 1988, 1990). If programs are to be responsive to the homeless severely mentally ill population, creative and flexible policies for including these people and providing appropriate alcohol and other drug abuse treatment must supplant the current policies of exclusion.

It is important to remember that for people with severe mental illnesses, the abuse of alcohol or other drugs places them at increased risk for homelessness. Thus, developing accessible treatment programs for dually diagnosed individuals may be an important means of preventing homelessness in the severely mentally ill population.

Health Care

> Ensuring access to health care for the homeless population should be part of a broad initiative to ensure access to health care for all those who are unable to pay. (Institute of Medicine 1988)

Experience gained through the Robert Wood Johnson Foundation–Pew Memorial Trust's Health Care for the Homeless Program in the 1980s underscores the importance of integrating mental health and physical health care services (Scanlan and Brickner et al. 1990). Homeless people with severe mental disorders more often than not have many other unattended health problems, ranging from life-threatening infectious diseases, such as acquired immunodeficiency syndrome (AIDS) or tuberculosis, to less serious disorders that interact with or complicate the diagnosis and/or treatment of their multiple illnesses. Thus, it is essential that these individuals have access to the full range of medical assessment, diagnosis, and treatment.

The acute need to educate homeless people about preventing human immunodeficiency virus (HIV) infection and AIDS, minimizing HIV transmission, and obtaining appropriate health care if infected and/or ill is only now gaining attention. Recent data from the Centers for Disease Control indicate that as many as 20 percent of the homeless population in certain sites are infected with the AIDS virus—a finding that, in the absence of more specific data, presumably holds for the homeless severely mentally ill population as well (Allen et al. 1991).

To meet the health care needs of this population, it is necessary to have health care providers serve homeless people in shelters, drop-in centers, and on the streets. Health care can be encouraged by using clinical nurse specialists and psychiatric nurse practitioners as members of outreach and integrated care management teams to plan, implement, and evaluate care. These providers should assist with and arrange access to all aspects of health care, including assessment, diagnosis, and treatment planning; emergency care; inpatient care (if needed); primary and preventive health care; and linkage to specialty services. Because treatment of some infectious and communicable diseases, particularly tuberculosis and its drug-resistant varieties, is protracted, direct supervision of medication therapies may be required. Homeless people who have severe mental disorders cannot maneuver a totally separate health care system; it must be integrated with the rest of their care.

Many poor people, including some who are homeless and severely mentally ill, use emergency rooms as a source of primary health care, a practice that is costly for the health care system and inefficient for the clientele. Alternate modes of financing and providing health care delivery for indigent populations—both urban and rural—need to be developed.

Income Support and Benefits

An immediate and urgent goal of all service provision must be to obtain all entitlements and benefits for which homeless mentally ill people are eligible. Many of these people live well below the poverty line or have no income at all, despite their eligibility for a variety of income-support programs. The vast majority need assistance in obtaining and retaining the benefits to which they are already entitled or for which they are eligible, especially food stamps and other nutritional programs, SSI, SSDI, Aid to Families with Dependent Children, State general assistance, local welfare assistance, and veterans' benefits.

The adequacy of benefits may well be an issue—with particular attention needed to providing benefits that enable decent housing and health/mental health/substance abuse care to be affordable and accessible to this population. There can be no debate, however, that access to benefits is essential and that even inadequate benefits are better than none. Service providers and benefit-paying agencies must work together to identify individuals who may be eligible for benefit programs, expedite agency access to information necessary to determine an individual's entitlements, and assist homeless mentally ill people in maintaining entitlements. Training and accurate information must be available to service providers to ensure that all those eligible are enrolled. Service providers and agencies also need to work together to find and train people outside of government to serve as representative payees for those people who are unable to manage their own funds.

Better coordination is needed of outreach efforts related to Federal entitlements, benefits, and programs for which poor severely mentally ill persons may be eligible. Having each individual program do its own outreach to severely mentally ill people who are homeless or at risk of homelessness is inefficient and confusing to clients. Coordinated outreach, such as the joint outreach effort between the Department of Veterans Affairs and the Social Security Administration, can save considerable time and expense.

Rehabilitation, Vocational Training, and Employment Assistance

To help people with severe mental illnesses—whether homeless or not— become and remain contributing members of society, rehabilitation, vocational training, and assistance in work settings are essential. These services must encompass the development or relearning of skills and competencies required for successful interpersonal and social functioning as well as those needed for specific vocational pursuits. Key services include assessment of goals, skills, and supports; linkage with vocational training, jobs, and other meaningful daytime activities; and opportunities to participate in supported employment, clubhouse programs, and recreational activities. Homeless people with a severe mental illness generally value these services, which are important to the process of recovery and can contribute both to self-esteem and self-support.

Psychosocial or social rehabilitation focuses on enhancing social and interpersonal skills that improve access to a social network and the emotional support its members can offer. Psychosocial programs provide training in activities of daily living, such as cooking, shopping, housekeeping, and budgeting. In rehabilitation of people with severe mental disorders, symptom and medication management receives strong emphasis . Learning about mental illness, the nature and meaning of symptoms, and methods of dealing with them is a key to helping these individuals become active, informed partners in rehabilitation. In addition, clubhouse rehabilitation models, with significant consumer involvement in design and management, can offer much-needed social, vocational, and employment opportunities.

Major obstacles to employment of people with severe mental illnesses result from their lack of currently marketable skills. Other problems arise from negative interactions with co-workers and supervisors, who may lack information about the nature of mental illnesses and the individual worker's strengths and limitations. Vocational training can increase employability and improve long-term prospects for avoiding homelessness. Employment assistance, including transitional, supportive, and other employment programs, must be designed to respond to the many difficulties faced by homeless people with a severe mental illness as they seek to enter or return to the work force.

Because the disabilities associated with mental illnesses are often cyclical, variable levels of support are required for homeless severely mentally ill individuals at different times. In general, compared with other homeless individuals, those with a severe mental illness require more flexible services (e.g., in sequence, duration, and amount) both in the initial stages of rehabilitation, vocational training, and employment assistance and over the long term. Another point is that improvement in social and vocational functioning can occur despite the recurrence of psychiatric symptoms.

Consumer and Family Involvement

Consumer Involvement

> The discovery of the self-help movement among mental health consumers, ex-patients and survivors can play a major role in the recovery process. The philosophy of choice, self-determination and involvement in one's rehabilitation has continued to be a crucial force in this burgeoning civil rights movement. Just within the last several years, consumers/ex-patients/survivors have become actively vocal in the development, operation and evaluation of mental health services, many of them user-run. (Van Tosh 1991)

Current and former consumers of mental health services constitute an invaluable but often overlooked resource in advocating and providing services for homeless people with severe mental illnesses. This underuse needs to be corrected immediately—through education to minimize stigma, through employment opportunities for these valuable allies in the provision of services to homeless mentally ill individuals, and through the encouragement of consumer-run programs for the target population. As noted by one consumer,

> The mental health system is beginning to realize the importance of empowerment of mental health consumers. Mental health systems and programs that involve consumers in their decision-making bodies benefit from and improve due to that involvement....Self-help, client-run programs offer that empowerment. In these programs, clients have the opportunity to help out, assist others, and become involved....Even the most well-funded, most comprehensive programs merely recycle people through homelessness when they do not empower their clients. With self-help, clients break the cycle of homelessness because they are empowered. (Harp 1991)

Several innovative programs across the country, many funded through NIMH and DOL demonstration grants, have shown the wisdom of utilizing consumers in engaging street people and encouraging their transition indoors.

Family Involvement

Like consumers, families of people with a severe mental illness constitute a potentially important but extremely underused resource in helping to prevent and overcome homelessness. Efforts to address the needs of the target population should include attention to enabling families to provide needed housing and care, when such an arrangement is mutually desirable. Giving families of severely mentally ill individuals access to crisis/emergency systems to help them cope with periodic episodes of acute illness, and offering respite services (e.g., the provision of adequate supervision of a mentally ill family member to allow families to attend to business matters or take vacations) might improve the ability of families to house and support their ill family member. People with a severe mental illness who live with their families may thus gain time to prepare for independent living and avoid the risks of homelessness stemming from precipitously leaving home. These people may also benefit from the provision of funding that could assist their families in financing living arrangements for them.

The legal principle of confidentiality protects important interests of privacy. However, for families and caregivers, confidentiality can be interpreted in a way that creates obstacles for communication and offers of support. Not involving families or community providers in aftercare planning from hospital or shelter settings can increase the chances that a formerly homeless mentally ill person will return to the streets. Given the importance of confidentiality as a principle in treating mental illnesses, it should not be abandoned lightly. If issues are dealt with sensitively and on a case-by-case basis, however, some obstacles can be circumvented. For example, a homeless mentally ill person's approval for releasing information to family members in the event of hospitalization could be obtained during less acutely ill periods.

Stigmatization of mentally ill people and their families must be reduced through public education (see Community and Public Education below). As one family member put it, "It is essential to educate those who work with homeless people with a severe mental illness that we families want to help. We are part of the team, not part of the problem" (J. Wild, personal communication, June 20, 1991).

Legal Protections in Clinical Care[7]

People who are severely mentally ill and homeless comprise a particularly vulnerable population in need of legal protections from many types of discrimination, mistreatment, and abuse. Services must be available to protect client and patient rights, to advocate (both at the individual and systems

---

[7] Much of the material in this section is based upon a paper by Paul Appelbaum, M.D. that was commissioned by the Task Force for this report.

levels) for improved access to appropriate care, and to promote consumer empowerment and choice. However, the role of the law in addressing the needs of these individuals is a matter of some controversy. Questions regarding the legal aspects of clinical care, the interface with the criminal justice system, and discriminatory zoning or housing access practices arise from the complex challenges of serving this population.

Systems of care for treating mentally ill people have been based on the premise that, in extreme circumstances, coercive treatment may be required. This assumption stems from observing that mentally ill people are at times incapable of making competent decisions about their need for care or that they present serious threats to their own well-being or the well-being of others. While the subgroup of homeless mentally ill people meeting these criteria appears to be relatively small, the proposals for expanding mechanisms for coercive care are numerous. These proposals come from caring family members or providers who are frustrated by their perceived inability to change this desperate living condition. They also come from less benevolent people who simply want the problematic people in their neighborhoods to disappear. Given the primacy of State law in most matters relating to mental health, decisions about changing these standards will, in all likelihood, be the responsibility of the States.

Although changes in commitment standards have been suggested as a remedy to these problems, there is no empirical evidence to support the belief that changes in civil commitment laws would provide a solution to the problems of homeless mentally ill persons. In fact, current laws are much less restrictive than is commonly believed. In addition, factors other than the law, such as the availability of alternative resources within the community, may influence commitment decisions. Certainly, if involuntary commitment laws are liberalized, no long-term benefits can be derived without an accompanying increase in resources to care for the newly designated population. In some communities, the paucity of voluntary inpatient beds forces practitioners to commit an individual who might otherwise voluntarily accept a period of hospital treatment.

Committing certain individuals to outpatient care may have some relevance for those homeless mentally ill individuals who relapse after stopping medications, and some individuals with co-occurring substance abuse disorders who respond to enforced abstinence with a marked reduction of disruptive behavior. This legal mechanism must be accompanied by the resources needed to monitor, track, and reach out to disengaged people.

For some homeless mentally ill people, their capacity for judgment can be episodically affected by their disease, rendering them unable to make decisions about specific aspects of their lives, such as treatment or financial matters. In these instances, the appointment of a guardian or other designated decisionmaker, such as a representative payee, is a useful approach. However, the availability of and access to such guardians are often limited, and once a guardian is identified, protections are critical to this and other guardianship processes to ensure that the homeless mentally ill person is not victimized.

Other Steps in Support of Improved Service Delivery

In addition to the essential components outlined above, improving services for the severely mentally ill homeless population requires enhancing community understanding of both homelessness and severe mental illness, enlarging the cadre of qualified and concerned persons available to work with the population, and continuing to expand and refine the knowledge base on homelessness and its relationship to mental illness.

Community and Public Education

Stigmatization, fear, and mistrust regarding people with severe mental illnesses—especially those who are also homeless—are commonplace in our Nation. Such reactions influence both the direct responses of community members to these individuals and the development of local, State, and Federal policies affecting them.

Educational activities of many types are essential to improve public understanding of the capabilities and needs of homeless and severely mentally ill persons, to improve community acceptance and reduce stigma, and to reduce community resistance and discrimination in access to housing and jobs. The Task Force also believes that neither passing new "anti-vagrancy" ordinances nor intensifying enforcement of existing laws is an appropriate response to people living on the streets or one that contributes to a more informed public understanding. Local communities, when adequately informed, can provide the kinds of opportunities and environments that support the rehabilitation and reintegration of severely mentally ill members who are homeless.

Extensive community education should make it clear that:

- The most visible people on the streets represent the worst-case scenario of what happens when very ill people are ignored and their mental illnesses untreated.

- Even these worst-case examples can be dramatically improved if given the proper care and resources.

- A properly functioning service system can bring about that improvement by reaching out to people on the streets, helping them obtain the care and services they need to function at their best, and placing and supporting them in appropriate residential settings.

51

- While many of the system's greatest failures are highly visible on the streets, its successes are easy to miss, because people who are successfully rehabilitated simply become co-workers, neighbors, and friends.

Human Resource Development

Providing the kind of integrated service system needed by homeless people with severe mental illnesses requires the development of new philosophies, new types of service workers, and the retraining of individuals currently working in the system. Properly trained health and allied health professionals are needed on the front lines where homeless people are served. Several approaches to this problem must be explored. First, academic programs as well as on-the-job training curricula should be developed to enhance essential knowledge and skills among professional and paraprofessional workers in health, mental health, social service, and housing-related agencies and organizations that serve this population. Those with health and mental health training need to understand the special characteristics and service needs of the homeless population, and those oriented toward work with homeless people or housing need a greater understanding of the symptoms and implications of severe mental illness.

Second, to expand the pool of front-line workers, special programs need to be developed to train consumers and indigenous workers to join outreach teams, where their background and skills are particularly useful. Third, to aid recruitment and retention of personnel who are effective in working with the target population, attractive salaries and career ladders must be made available, and program planners and leaders must recognize and avert the strong potential for burnout among front-line workers. In addition, the traditional training systems and their accrediting mechanisms for health care, mental health, and social work should offer incentives for the acquisition of cultural competence by nonminority service providers.

Recognizing that many other professional and paraprofessional groups have intermittent but influential contacts with homeless severely mentally ill people, we would share the recommendation of a State mental health commissioner: "There is a need to cross-train staff in other agencies (e.g., police, shelter providers, soup kitchen operators) to identify mental illnesses and respond to the needs of mentally ill persons appropriately" (Bevilacqua 1991). Finally, the voluntary sector of our society serves as an important resource for the provision of services to homeless people. This sector should be included in any efforts to recruit and train workers and to increase staff knowledge and efficacy in dealing with homeless people who have severe mental illnesses.

Research and Evaluation

The findings of the Task Force reflect a striking consensus—based on both research and practical experience—concerning what must be done. But these guidelines remain general and relatively imprecise. The McKinney Act has authorized funding for three research demonstration programs (managed by NIMH, NIAAA, and DOL); these programs provide valuable information on the design, delivery, and efficacy of essential service elements for homeless mentally ill persons, including those with co-occurring alcohol and/or other drug disorders. However, substantial additional research is needed to provide more precise information that can be used to improve services for the homeless severely mentally ill population and maximize the effectiveness of existing approaches to treatment and rehabilitation.

Just as recent advances in clinical and basic research have contributed to significant progress in the assessment and treatment of mental disorders, so too must the development of systems of care be guided by the results of rigorous scientific inquiry. We need to know more about what works, for whom, and under what circumstances. A research plan to address the needs of severely mentally ill persons was prepared by the National Mental Health Advisory Council entitled, *Caring for People with Severe Mental Disorders: A National Plan of Research to Improve Services* (NIMH 1991c). Building on this plan and focusing on the unique needs of those severely mentally ill persons who are homeless will encourage the systematic identification of best practices.

With the broad range of treatment and housing services required to address homelessness and severe mental illness, research initiatives will benefit from collaboration between academic researchers and public-sector agencies in the planning and conduct of research. In addition, Federal efforts, such as the Interagency Council on the Homeless Work Group on Data Collection, can complement State, local, and private efforts.

Both process and outcome evaluations are needed on an ongoing basis to determine the effectiveness and costs of interventions for homeless severely mentally ill people and to refine our current approaches based on the best available knowledge. We agree with the observations of our Advisory Committee, who stated that:

> ... research strategies should be a central component [of developing a comprehensive plan for homeless mentally ill persons], with project budgets specifically designated for the evaluation. The highest standard of scientific rigor should be employed in designing the evaluation research. Individual project evaluations should be coordinated nationally in an attempt to employ a common set of approaches and methods that may be used to compare and contrast client outcomes resulting from differing program models. (Surles et al. 1991)

Photo ©JOHN KEITH

Action Steps and Recommendations

Homelessness in America must come to an end. We believe it can, even among homeless people least able to help themselves: those disabled by severe mental illnesses. The action steps and recommendations presented here are predicated on the assumption that ending homelessness among the Nation's severely mentally ill population will require strong leadership and vigorous action at every level—local, State, and Federal, as well as the private sector.

We stress the Federal role, however, because it reflects the special perspective and expertise of the Task Force members, and because we believe that appropriate Federal leadership can stimulate the changes required to end homelessness in America. Our Task Force provides an unusual opportunity because our members can directly effect significant policy changes in their respective agencies and departments. Thus, in the first major section to follow, we describe vital steps the Federal Government can and will take—in many cases already has begun—to remove barriers and strengthen incentives to vastly improve services for the homeless severely mentally ill population. These steps are designed to promote systems integration, improve outreach and access to existing programs, expand housing options and alternative services, and generate and disseminate knowledge and information.

Any successful effort to end homelessness among the severely mentally ill population, however, must be pluralistic, involving Federal, State, and local governments as well as providers, family members, voluntary organizations, and mental health consumers. Thus, we also present recommendations to State and local governments, as well as the private sector.

We realize that the systemic factors underlying the problems of homeless mentally ill persons are so complicated, interrelated, and interjurisdictional that they are not remediable simply by quick fixes. A sustained effort will be required. Therefore, we have agreed that the Interagency Council on the Homeless will, within 60 days from the issuance of this report, incorporate into the *Federal Plan to Help End Homelessness* the action steps and recommendations outlined below, as well as a strategy for monitoring and tracking the timeliness of their completion. Additionally, a committee of the Council will be constituted to work with NIMH and other organizations to provide integrated Federal oversight to address the needs of homeless severely mentally ill persons on an ongoing basis.

We believe that although there is no single remedy or cure for homelessness across our Nation—especially among extremely disabled populations such as those with severe mental illnesses—each community can discover and develop its own effective solutions. The action steps and recommendations presented here should hasten the process of discovery.

Federal Action Steps[8]

We, the members of the Task Force on Homelessness and Severe Mental Illness, find it unacceptable that our most vulnerable and disabled citizens, in both urban and rural America, live in the most precarious and threatening life situations. A problem of such magnitude and severity demands an immediate response. In searching for specific Federal action steps that could be undertaken by the departments represented on the Task Force, we have carefully scrutinized and seized opportunities currently available to us with the "stroke of a pen" to promote systems integration, improve access, and remove impediments to housing, treatment, and supports. In addition, we have proposed a number of action steps requiring congressional support.

Promote Systems Integration

The Task Force reached broad consensus that ending homelessness among severely mentally ill people requires an integrated system of care that offers access to essential services and to affordable and safe housing. Efforts must be made to put such systems in place in communities across the Nation. To provide needed leadership, HHS, in collaboration with HUD, DOL, DOEd, VA, and the USDA, will make Access to Community Care and Effective Services and Supports (ACCESS) grants to States and local governments to provide incentives for developing comprehensive and integrated systems of treatment, housing, and support for homeless people with severe mental illnesses. This specific initiative will be part of a larger systematic effort to review and make improvements to the existing array of Federal programs and services.

1. ACCESS Initiative

The long-term goal of the ACCESS initiative is to foster enduring partnerships that will improve the integration of existing Federal, State, local, and

---

[8] The Federal action steps presented here were developed by Task Force members, in conjunction with their respective departments, to improve the housing and services available to homeless people with severe mental illnesses. They include new initiatives as well as efforts to strengthen the accessibility and impact of existing programs relevant to this population. For more specific information on the programs mentioned here and on other current Federal activities relevant to the homeless population, we recommend *The 1990 Annual Report of the Interagency Council on the Homeless.*

voluntary services to homeless people with severe mental illnesses. The more immediate goal is to test promising approaches to services integration within communities that require immediate assistance in ending homelessness among the severely mentally ill individuals residing in their shelters, jails, public transportation settings, parks, and on their streets.

To be eligible for an ACCESS grant, a State, working with one or more specific target communities, will be required to develop, implement, and participate in the evaluation of a plan to improve integration of all existing and potential resources relevant to the needs of homeless severely mentally ill people in those communities. (At a minimum, this plan would include all of the elements identified in the preceding section entitled, Essential Service System Components.)

Applicants will be asked to propose methods for improving service system integration, at both State and local levels, and will be required to identify a strategy for promoting systems integration at each target site. Because the ACCESS grants are intended to test models that could be adapted and used in other communities nationally, a sound plan for evaluation and monitoring will be required. In addition, HHS (NIMH) will oversee a large-scale evaluation to assess whether services integration significantly enhances client outcome over and above the provision of additional services.

In designing their systems integration plans, potential applicants will be able to take advantage of extensive federally supported pre-application technical assistance. Such assistance will include general information on the service needs of the homeless mentally ill population, advice on preparing applications and on using mainstream and targeted Federal programs and relevant Federal waiver authorities, and suggestions for evaluation methodology.

Successful applicants will have the added opportunity of participating in an array of technical assistance, training, expedited review of waiver requests, and other partnership activities associated with the initiative. These will include, for example, HHS (Health Care Financing Administration—HCFA) working with the sites concerning innovative uses of Medicaid, such as managed care and home- and community-based services; targeted case management; and clinical and rehabilitation services. Other examples include SSA's provision of training and other technical assistance concerning the eligibility rules, processing, and procedures with respect to Social Security and the SSI programs, such as expedited review of eligibility claims, and the setting of income and resource levels to allow individuals to establish and maintain a permanent place of residence. (Complete information on the ACCESS initiative and application procedures will appear shortly in the *Federal Register*.)

Additional Steps to Promote Systems Integration

In addition to the ACCESS initiative, the following steps will be taken by Federal departments and agencies to promote systems integration:

2.   The inadequate quality of discharge planning from institutional settings to communities has been identified as a factor contributing to homelessness among severely mentally ill persons. Often, this occurs because clinicians and hospital administrators are faced with the dilemma of choosing between unnecessarily prolonged hospital stays or releasing individuals before appropriate arrangements have been made to meet their needs for community-based housing, treatment, and supports. To improve this critical transition, HHS will explore options to enhance discharge planning policies and procedures (formal transfer of comprehensive care of a patient) from mental and acute care hospitals to a community.

In addition, HHS (NIMH) and DOJ will explore options to improve the planning process for release of mentally ill persons from jails and prisons to ensure necessary continuity of care.

Also, the VA will continue to establish criteria for identifying those persons in VA programs who are most at risk of becoming homeless after discharge, and will further develop its strategies for pre-discharge homelessness prevention interventions.

3.   HUD and HHS will jointly encourage coordination in the development of State mental health plans (Comprehensive Mental Health Services Plans) and State and local housing (Comprehensive Housing Affordability Strategy) plans, so that services to homeless people with a severe mental illness might be implemented in a comprehensive manner.

4.   HUD will propose legislative language that would add a new section to Subtitle A of Title IV (Housing Assistance) of the McKinney Act requiring all project operators receiving housing assistance under Title IV to participate in a local program coordinating committee designed to coordinate social services, health services, education, job training, and housing. The objective would be to develop more effective linkages between housing for homeless individuals and families and supportive services provided through both public and private programs.

5.   HUD will issue a notice to States and over 870 cities and urban counties explaining how Community Development Block Grant funds may be used to match other Federal programs and fund such activities as public services, homelessness prevention activities, mental health services, acquisition and rehabilitation of emergency and transitional shelters, single-room-occupancy facilities, and other permanent housing models that address the needs of the homeless mentally ill population.

6. The rehabilitation and employment of homeless persons with a severe mental illness are challenging issues that extend beyond the boundaries of any one system. Building upon current agency activities, the Departments of Labor, Health and Human Services, and Education will establish a Memorandum of Understanding to guide collaborative efforts to address both knowledge gaps and policy/program development in meeting the rehabilitation/job training needs of the homeless mentally ill population.

7. DOL will review wage and hour laws and regulations to determine whether enforcement imposes unreasonable barriers to the development of supported and transitional work opportunities for the homeless severely mentally ill population.

8. Because family members care deeply for their severely mentally ill relatives who may be lost on the streets, HHS, HUD, and DOJ will explore ways to improve family member/guardian access to information concerning missing and possibly homeless, mentally ill relatives. In addition, these departments will examine ways to improve communication among families, providers, and law enforcement officials.

9. HHS (NIMH) and DOJ will develop a Memorandum of Understanding to stimulate approaches to divert to appropriate treatment settings those homeless people with a severe mental illness who are inappropriately placed in jails.

Improve Outreach and Access to Existing Programs

A major finding of the Task Force was the recognition that existing Federal programs and benefits relevant—and often essential—to homeless people with a severe mental illness are not being fully utilized by many States and local communities. We propose measures to overcome these problems and ensure that Federal resources reach their intended target populations.

10. HHS (SSA) will continue to increase outreach activities to homeless individuals, especially to homeless mentally ill persons. SSA will do this in part through its SSI outreach demonstration projects, which seek to demonstrate effective, efficient, ongoing, and transferable approaches for identifying potentially eligible individuals, assisting them through the application process, helping them continue to receive SSI benefits as long as they remain eligible, and linking them with other available and appropriate financial benefits and social services that will improve the quality of their lives and help them obtain the greatest possible measure of independence.

11. HHS (NIMH) will stringently monitor and enforce the existing legislative mandate in P.L. 99-660 (State Mental Health Planning Act), which requires that States establish and implement a program of outreach to,

and services for, individuals with a severe mental illness who are homeless.

12. A basic component of the VA Homeless Chronically Mentally Ill (HCMI) Veterans Program is assertive outreach to homeless mentally ill veterans in shelters, at soup kitchens, and on the streets. The VA will expand outreach to local homelessness coalitions and nonprofit organizations at its HCMI and Domiciliary Care for Homeless Veterans Program sites.

13. The VA and SSA will implement a joint pilot project to improve outreach to homeless veterans regarding SSI and SSDI benefits. An additional goal will be to expedite the processing of their eligibility claims.

14. HUD will consider revising regulations to allow the combined use of Section 8 rental certificates in its Supportive Housing Demonstration Program.

15. To aid residents leaving HUD-supported Transitional Housing facilities, HUD will propose legislation to provide Section 8 vouchers or certificates as incentives for transition from homelessness to independent living. Under this proposal, Section 8(d)(a)(A) of the United States Housing Act of 1937 would be amended to add a provision requiring public housing agencies to give preference for participation to individuals and families who are ready to move to independent living from the Transitional Housing program assisted under Title IV of the McKinney Act.

16. DOL has proposed to Congress to make homeless persons one of the specified target groups for eligibility under the Job Training Partnership Act (JTPA) Title IIA. This change would help facilitate service to the homeless severely mentally ill population. If enacted, DOL (Employment and Training Administration) will prepare appropriate technical assistance materials for the JTPA system and work with States and local service providers to allow greater flexibility to permit expanded service to the homeless severely mentally ill population.

17. DOEd will designate severely mentally ill persons as a focus group for service by all relevant departmental programs.

Expand Housing Options and Alternative Services

The service system for homeless people with severe mental illnesses is evolving as research and practical experience offer promising new approaches to the provision of needed housing and supportive services. The following recommendations are intended to expand the range of alternatives available to homeless people with severe mental illnesses.

Safe Havens

In most localities, there is a paucity of residential alternatives available to the most disabled and difficult-to-reach portion of the homeless mentally ill population currently residing on the streets and in temporary shelters. As described in the Essential Service Components section under Safe Havens, many of these individuals would take advantage of small, secure, low-demand, safe havens, which would provide basic life supports and offer stable housing and assistance in linking these individuals to more specialized services.

18. HUD will propose to Congress a new, competitive demonstration program of safe havens designed to determine the feasibility of providing very low-cost stable housing for homeless mentally ill persons who are currently unwilling or unable to participate in existing housing programs that provide comprehensive supportive services designed to foster self-sufficiency. It is hoped that, after living in the stable environment of a safe haven for a while and coming to trust people operating the facility, residents will be more willing and able to be engaged in treatment and supportive service programs and will start to move toward greater self-sufficiency. However, agreeing to participate in such programs would not be required. Eligible program activities would include rehabilitation and operating costs, such as administration, furnishings, equipment, utilities, security, maintenance, repair, and case management. Grants would be awarded competitively and would include operating costs for a 5-year period, with the possibility of renewals for additional years.

Additional Steps to Expand Housing Options and Alternative Services

19. The HUD Shelter Plus Care (S+C) program provides flexible rental assistance for a wide array of living arrangements, including SROs, group homes, and individual apartments. HUD is seeking congressional approval to reprogram funds for the Tenant Rental Assistance component of the S+C program in 1992 and will seek full funding of the program in 1993.

20. To simplify administration of the S+C program, HUD will recommend to Congress amending the McKinney Act so that the existing three components of the program would be folded into one offering three types of rental assistance—tenant-based, project-based, and sponsor-based—which will provide more flexibility and responsiveness to local needs and conditions. The funding of the Section 8/SRO Moderate Rehabilitation program would be completely transferred into an expanded Shelter Plus Care/SRO program.

21. HUD is seeking congressional approval to permit community housing development organizations to assume ownership of substantially vacant public housing projects that are owned by "troubled" housing authorities. HUD would provide funds for the rehabilitation of the projects and for a transitional subsidy of the projects, where necessary, for up to 5 years.

    In addition, HUD would provide an incremental voucher to the Public Housing Authorities (PHAs) for every unit in the project to be sold. In a parallel but separate initiative, HUD is seeking legislative approval that would allow PHAs to lease vacant, underutilized units to public or private social service agencies that are able to provide supportive services to special needs populations.

22. In fiscal year 1992, HOME program funds will be available to non-profit intermediaries who, in turn, will provide technical assistance and training to community housing development organizations. HUD will seek to ensure that HOME funds are also available to developers of special needs housing. Such assistance would cover staff development support, financial management support, operating support, and other needs provided in-house or through consultants.

23. HHS (HCFA) will encourage and assist States to make full use of all current Medicaid program service authorities in the design of innovative packages of services for Medicaid-eligible homeless severely mentally ill persons. This package could include mandatory Medicaid services, optional services (e.g., targeted case management), and waivers to include services not otherwise available under the regular Medicaid program, such as homemaker services, home health aide services, personal care services, case management, adult day health, habilation, and respite care.

24. HHS (SSA) will continue to support the expeditious completion of the SSI Modernization Project, an initiative established by Commissioner Gwendolyn King in the spring of 1990. The purpose of this project is to undertake a comprehensive review of the SSI program to determine how well the program is meeting and will continue to meet the needs of the population it is intended to serve. The project has received public testimony from many individuals, including representatives of the homeless mentally ill population. In spring of 1992, SSA will publish for public comment the individual points of view of experts assisting the project. SSA will consider all comments and determine appropriate directions for the SSI program.

25. HUD's surplus property contacts in each field office will identify Title V Federal Surplus Property Program and Federal Housing Administration properties located in or near urban centers that are appropriate for use by homeless providers. These HUD contacts

will work with State homeless coordinators, local government officials, and administrators of nonprofit organizations in advertising these properties to organizations providing services to homeless mentally ill persons.

26. In fiscal year 1992, HUD will set aside 750 Section 8 housing vouchers to be used in conjunction with a VA-funded community-oriented clinical case management initiative at 19 VA Medical Centers. This HUD–VA Supported Housing Initiative will monitor and assess the development of longer term housing possibilities with appropriate continued treatment for needy veterans who complete the 90-day VA HCMI residential treatment program as well as other homeless and mentally ill veterans.

    The evaluation component of this initiative will assess the implementation of the program at each site and measure the effectiveness of varying combinations of housing and support services in assisting this target population.

27. The VA will develop and expand the Comprehensive Work Therapy/ Therapeutic Residence Program for homeless and at-risk veterans with a mental illness and/or substance abuse problems and will increase from 30 to 50 the number of homes purchased for transitional group residences.

28. HHS (NIMH and Health Resources Services Administration) will seek to broaden the definition of psychiatric health professional shortage areas and medical/mental health underservice areas to increase the number of psychiatrists, psychologists, psychiatric nurses, and social workers providing mental health services within Health Care for the Homeless projects.

29. To expand the cadre of mental health professionals trained to work with homeless mentally ill persons, HHS (NIMH) will add homeless populations as a priority group in Requests for Applications for professional and institutional training grants supporting the education of psychiatrists, psychologists, social workers, psychiatric nurses, and family therapists. Special efforts will be made to encourage the participation of racial/ethnic minority persons.

30. HHS (NIMH) will issue a Request for Applications under its State Human Resource Development program to encourage retraining of State personnel to provide outreach and integrated care management to homeless mentally ill individuals. Retraining efforts will include information on pre-release agreements (to begin timely initiation of SSI benefits) and requirements for continuation of benefits during temporary periods of hospitalization.

Generate and Disseminate Knowledge and Information

Technical Assistance

Substantial resources, both public and private, are currently available to improve the lives of homeless people, including those who are severely mentally ill. However, many communities and eligible individuals are not making use of them—especially those offered by the Federal Government—because they are unaware that such resources are available. Communities often are discouraged from seeking funding because of misunderstandings or the actual difficulty of complying with confusing and sometimes contradictory regulations. Gaining access to, and making effective use of, existing resources are urgent and essential steps in developing comprehensive services for homeless people with severe mental illness.

We, the Task Force on Homelessness and Severe Mental Illness, are impressed by the need for better communication among Federal agencies, State and local providers, and consumers. We are committed to coordinating the technical assistance efforts of our respective agencies and departments as an essential contribution to integrating services. The following action steps are designed to address critical information gaps and promote the coordination required to close them. A lead department/agency has been identified for each of the following activities:

31. The Interagency Council on the Homeless will enhance its capacity to provide professional and technical assistance relevant to the homeless severely mentally ill population and to refer requests for information to appropriate programs within the Federal Government. Specifically, the Council will issue a policy guidance to its 10 regional coordinators and respective regional interagency councils to use its 110 members to assist in site visits to identify exemplary programs or issues of concern relevant to the homeless severely mentally ill population. In addition, the Council will encourage grassroots support in communities and neighborhoods through distribution of publications directed to various groups.

32. The Council will provide training and disseminate technical materials to State and local agencies working with the target population to improve outreach and assessment techniques.

33. The Council will provide technical assistance to States and communities to market the availability of federally owned housing (HUD, VA, Resolution Trust Corporation, and the Department of Defense) for this population.

34. In January 1990, the Secretaries of HUD and HHS signed a Memorandum of Understanding with the ultimate goal of more effectively helping poor families and individuals move toward independent living and

economic independence. The homeless mentally ill population was identified as one of the three target groups to be assisted by this effort. NIMH and HUD have been working collaboratively to sponsor joint activities that include pilot projects in communities, policy review and development, research and evaluation, and technical assistance and training. Based on the findings of the Task Force and building upon this ongoing collaboration between the two Departments, HUD and HHS will undertake a major technical assistance effort to aid States, regional HUD and HHS staff, local housing agencies, and mental health agencies in developing programs of housing linked with services for severely mentally ill persons.

Responding to two immediate priorities identified through this process, HUD and HHS will develop a technical assistance monograph that describes and promotes the coordination of case management/supportive services with both Transitional and Permanent components of the HUD Supportive Housing Demonstration program. HUD and HHS will also develop and distribute a monograph of case studies to illustrate how mentally ill persons can be successfully integrated into elderly public housing.

35. HHS (NIMH) will implement a national education initiative aimed at State and community leaders; treatment, service, and housing professionals; and the general public focused on the needs of the homeless mentally ill population and appropriate responses. NIMH will disseminate public information on homelessness and severe mental illness.

36. HHS (NIMH) will identify exemplary comprehensive projects that integrate housing and support services for homeless severely mentally ill persons and will disseminate information on how they were developed and how they can be adapted to other communities. NIMH will expand dissemination activities of the National Resource Center on Homelessness and Mental Illness, which is co-funded by NIMH and HUD, to assist housing, treatment, and service providers in addressing the needs of the target population.

37. During 1991, HHS (HCFA) implemented a "streamlined" process for States to apply for Medicaid Home and Community Based Services Waivers and Freedom of Choice Waivers. This effort provided States with a structured format to use in applying for these waivers that will result in a more efficient and timely process. Renewals for existing waivers have also been simplified. HCFA has received many positive comments on the new application process and will continue to work with States to make further improvements as needed.

In addition, HCFA will provide States with information and follow-up technical assistance on Medicaid program options to serve the homeless severely mentally ill population. Future workshops with Federal Medicaid staff and State mental health staff will be conducted.

38. The Projects for Assistance in Transition from Homelessness (PATH) Formula Grant program administered by NIMH provides funds to States for services for homeless mentally ill individuals and permits up to 20 percent of grant funds to be used for a set of specified housing costs. These grants are intended to promote coordination of treatment, housing, and support services. The grants also require services to meet the needs of dually diagnosed homeless persons. HHS (NIMH) will provide technical assistance and support ongoing networking among PATH State recipients to maximize use of eligible funds for integrated service delivery.

39. HHS (NIMH) will provide technical assistance to Protection and Advocacy Program grantees to improve knowledge and understanding of the legal rights and needs of homeless mentally ill individuals.

40. HHS (Alcohol, Drug Abuse and Mental Health Administration— ADAMHA) will undertake a national community education initiative to educate people about the homeless population with co-occurring alcohol, drug, and mental disorders. This initiative will take the form of additional efforts in jointly funded research and research demonstration programs as well as joint efforts in dissemination of information through publications and conferences.

41. HHS (ADAMHA) will hold regional meetings to disseminate research findings and provide technical assistance to service providers who are working with mentally ill homeless individuals who have co-occurring alcohol and/or other drug problems.

42. HHS (ADAMHA) will provide technical assistance to State ADMS Block Grantees to improve access to treatment programs and to expand services to homeless mentally ill and dually diagnosed individuals.

43. HHS (SSA) will continue to work with representatives of State agencies and other organizations of treatment providers to offer technical assistance regarding provisions of the SSI program that might be more fully utilized to: (1) prevent homelessness (e.g., pre-release provisions), (2) ensure continuation of payments to those individuals who are temporarily in medical or psychiatric institutions, and (3) encourage providers to become or help find representative payees. In addition, as SSA field offices develop successful practices for outreach to homeless mentally ill individuals, these will be shared with all offices for replication.

44. HUD will propose to set aside up to 2 percent of its Supportive Housing Demonstration Program to provide technical assistance to local communities and nonprofit organizations to develop more innovative approaches to end homelessness in their communities.

45. HUD will issue a monograph that explains how State and local governments may use Community Development Block Grant funding for the repair and renovation of surplus Title V and HUD-Owned Single Properties that can be used for housing homeless mentally ill persons.

46. HUD will develop a monograph on the Section 8 program for mental health providers, families, and consumers that will illustrate how the vouchers can be obtained and used by severely mentally ill persons.

47. DOL will document service strategies used by DOL demonstration program grantees that serve the homeless mentally ill population exclusively. DOL and its national evaluation and technical assistance contractor will then use these materials in program newsletters and will use additional methods to assist other program grantees to serve the homeless severely mentally ill population more effectively.

48. DOEd will develop, in collaboration with its funded Research and Training Centers in Mental Health, a major technical assistance program for States, localities, community mental health centers, and others concerning the rehabilitation of homeless severely mentally ill persons.

49. HHS (NIMH) will support the development of model curricula for training professionals and paraprofessionals (including consumers) to provide services and outreach to homeless mentally ill persons.

50. HHS (NIMH) will support the development of a "best practices" guide to improve the quality of psychiatric services delivered to homeless severely mentally ill people.

Research and Evaluation

The Task Force held discussions with many service providers, consumers, and advocates focusing on the unmet needs of homeless mentally ill individuals. A recurring theme was the need for a better understanding of the types of services that are effective for this diverse group of individuals. The following action steps are designed to address this knowledge gap.

51. Building on Task Force priorities and earlier McKinney research demonstration efforts, and consistent with the NIMH National Plan of Research to Improve Services, HHS (NIMH) will sponsor the development, evaluation, refinement, testing, and dissemination of exemplary models of integrated services for the homeless severely mentally ill population. Research on access to care, utilization, organization, costs, financing, and outcomes of service delivery systems will be promoted. The objectives of these efforts are to improve clinical care and outcomes, increase efficiency and effectiveness, and inform mental health and health care policy.

In addition, the study of subgroups of the severely mentally ill homeless population, such as women, minorities, and individuals with co-occurring substance abuse disorders, AIDS, or other physical illnesses, will be supported.

52. HHS (NIMH) will fund a national Research Center on Homelessness and Mental Illness, which will be devoted to such research issues as risk factors for homelessness among the severely mentally ill population, the incidence of violence among homeless mentally ill individuals, the essential components of integrated care management (e.g., what it is, who performs it, and how costs are saved), and experimental approaches to overcoming services fragmentation. Additional research areas might include the efficacy of incentives to maintain mentally ill persons in home-based settings, the impact of integrating homeless severely mentally ill individuals with other groups in subsidized housing (e.g., elderly, disabled, and low income, especially in settings now underused), and models for matching care/treatment to housing type. Critical clinical and policy issues for research include the incidence of HIV infection and AIDS, the risks/benefits of HIV testing in the homeless severely mentally ill population, and the impact of seropositivity on shelter access.

53. HHS (NIMH and the Office for Treatment Improvement, ADAMHA) will fund an integrated treatment center to assess the efficacy of this approach in treating homeless mentally ill persons with co-occurring alcohol and/or other drug disorders. Comprehensive psychosocial and psychiatric assessments, together with appropriate medical interventions, would be supported through a central intake, assessment, and referral unit. Housing, vocational rehabilitation, and other essential elements of an integrated system of care would be ensured.

54. HHS (NIMH) will award competitive grant supplements to existing research centers on schizophrenia, housing, rural issues, and financing issues to encourage a focus on minority, organizational, and rehabilitation issues relevant to the homeless mentally ill population.

55. HHS (ADAMHA and SSA) will co-sponsor research and research demonstrations on outreach models, representative payees, and work incentives to generate knowledge on effective methods to increase self-sufficiency among homeless mentally ill individuals.

56. HHS (NIMH and HCFA) will actively pursue opportunities to co-sponsor research on Medicaid/Medicare coverage of mental health services.

57. HHS (NIMH) will develop a competitive supplement program for adding a homeless focus within ongoing research projects funded under the National Plan for Research on Schizophrenia (this may include secondary analyses of data). Research issues explored under this initiative

include the development of more acceptable and effective medications for use in community treatment of people with severe mental illness.

58. The VA will continue to synthesize its research data and disseminate findings regarding the effectiveness of alternative outreach and treatment methods for homeless veterans.

Recommendations to State and Local Governments

States and localities have statutory responsibilities for the design, funding, and operation of treatment, housing, and social welfare services to homeless and severely mentally ill persons and are accountable for the successes and failures of these efforts. These components of the public sector have not only the most direct exposure to the problems associated with homelessness and severe mental illness, but also the clearest understanding of the specific responses required of particular communities. Moreover, State and local governments are also relied upon for providing leadership. With the relative absence of a strong constituency for the target population and the complexity of the funding, administration, and delivery mechanisms for essential services, the political will of State and local leaders (as well as other citizens) to address these problems becomes a major determinant in ending homelessness among severely mentally ill persons. Specifically, authorities with responsibility for treating mental illness, for housing, and for support services need to specify action steps to develop integrated and comprehensive solutions. Therefore, we, the Task Force, recommend that the following steps (also being pursued at the Federal level) be followed by each State and locality.

Promote Systems Integration

- *Establish lead responsibility* for the housing and ongoing care, treatment, and rehabilitation of severely mentally ill people, including those who are homeless.

- *Develop structural mechanisms* (such as coordinating bodies, task forces, public mental health authorities, memoranda of understanding, and letters of agreement) *to improve the planning for and integration of services and housing* for people with a severe mental illness who are homeless or at imminent risk of homelessness.

- Outline respective roles and responsibilities regarding *coordination of hospital and community programs* so that discharge planning includes adequate attention to the housing, income support, rehabilitation, and other social welfare needs of severely mentally ill persons as well as notification to community treatment programs and families of the current residence of individuals who have given informed consent.

- *Identify gaps in resources* to ensure that planning and services development are strategically targeted to meet the most urgent needs for housing, care, and treatment.

- *Encourage collaboration between mental health and criminal justice systems* so that severely mentally ill persons are diverted from inappropriate placement in jails and prisons.

- *Coordinate alcohol, drug abuse, and mental health services programs* so that homeless people with co-occurring severe mental illness and an alcohol and/or other drug abuse disorder are appropriately assessed, diagnosed, and treated.

Improve Outreach and Access to Existing Programs

- *Gather data* on the extent of homelessness and severe mental illnesses in communities.

- *Expand outreach efforts* to ensure that benefits and services are available to individuals who would have inordinate difficulty seeking out these resources on their own.

- *Review eligibility and application processes* for public programs and resources to ensure that they do not inadvertently exclude or discriminate against homeless or severely mentally ill persons.

- *Review existing laws, regulations, and policies* (such as civil commitment statutes, vagrancy laws, health and safety codes, and zoning ordinances) and modify them to ensure access of severely mentally ill homeless individuals to appropriate services and to eliminate unnecessarily punitive laws.

- *Protect and advocate* for the rights of homeless severely mentally ill individuals in transitional institutions, shelters, and permanent housing.

Expand Housing Options and Alternative Services

- *Provide policy leadership and fiscal incentives* to end the tragedy of homelessness among severely mentally ill persons.

- *Develop, fund, operate, monitor, and evaluate a full range of programs* required to meet the needs of severely mentally ill people who are homeless and to prevent homelessness among those who are severely mentally ill.

- *Ensure quality of care* by monitoring the appropriateness and effectiveness of treatment and care, in both human and economic terms, including the establishment of standards of care and professional practice as well as procedures for the inspection and monitoring of safety, fire, and sanitation compliance in hospital- and community-based settings.

- *Educate, train, and retrain the mental health, housing, and human service work force* to improve the availability of appropriate treatment and care, involving collaboration between universities and public mental health, housing, and social welfare programs.

Generate and Disseminate Knowledge and Information

- *Catalogue all relevant resources*—both across levels of government and across mental health, housing, and other human agencies—that might potentially be applied to meet the needs of the target population, and make this information readily available to providers, consumers, and their families.

- *Educate and inform the public* about the tragic circumstances and compelling needs of homeless mentally ill people as well as the potential roles that communities and ordinary citizens can play in successful rehabilitation and community integration and the variety of Federal discretionary and entitlement programs that are available to assist homeless mentally ill persons.

Recommendations to the Private Sector

Corporations, academic institutions, religious and charitable institutions, community and private foundations, and individual citizens have all historically played an important role in addressing the needs of homeless mentally ill individuals. That role is gaining even greater prominence as State and local governments struggle, often with shrinking budgets, to meet increasing needs and demands from diverse groups for health, mental health, substance abuse, and social welfare services. Thus, private-sector initiatives focused on homeless mentally ill persons are an essential component of efforts to address the national tragedy described in this report.

In responding to emergency needs and advocating for more systemic service improvements, the flexibility and commitment of the voluntary sector complement the necessarily more measured pace of government activities and initiatives. Private-sector contributions of volunteer time, seed money, matching funds, and other support are critical to the success of any attempt to develop a community-based system of care and often serve to leverage additional contributions.

Foundation-initiated programs, such as the Robert Wood Johnson-Pew Memorial Trust Health Care for the Homeless Program, have served to focus national attention on the needs of homeless individuals. They have also stimulated interest, both in the Congress and in the Administration, in the longer term Federal funding of very innovative and successful models of care.

The National Alliance to End Homelessness (1991) has recently published an excellent book highlighting ways in which individuals, families, and businesses can make a difference. The White House has also identified home-less persons as a target population for the *Points of Light* initiative, recogniz-ing the significant roles of volunteers in often dramatically improving the lives of homeless individuals.

While the structural causes of homelessness cannot be solved by the pri-vate sector alone and, in fact, demand governmental intervention, the Task Force has identified the following areas as particularly appropriate for future efforts among the private sector:

Provide Leadership at National, State, and Local Levels

Private-sector attention, endorsement, and talent can serve as a catalyst to improve systems of care for the homeless severely mentally ill population. These organizations and individuals who best understand the problems and barriers affecting local communities can spark the cooperative actions needed to overcome them.

Foster Public Awareness and Education

Widespread stigma and community resistance still need to be overcome if we are to meet the needs of homeless mentally ill individuals. Private-sector organizations—including mental health, housing, and homeless advocates—working with the media and local individuals and organizations in their com-munities can play a critical role in educating their neighbors about the problem of homelessness and mental illness.

Contribute Resources

Meeting the needs of the homeless severely mentally ill population and pre-venting homelessness will continue to challenge the resources and resourcefulness of all segments of our society. Continued investments of pri-vate-sector resources are essential if communities, States, and the Nation at large are to truly end homelessness among our severely mentally ill neighbors.

Epilogue

As part of its deliberations, the Task Force and its Advisory Committee met with many formerly homeless individuals who have been disabled by severe mental illnesses. These individuals described their own successful struggles to overcome their disability and homelessness. They once led lives not unlike those of James Lee, Scarlet McCaffrey, Benjamin Draper, Michael Dodge, and Gladys Williams, described earlier in this report. Each person's story was unique, but the essential themes were similar. As one individual explained, "People in my community were willing and able to offer the many kinds of ongoing assistance I needed to pull myself together. I'm still struggling to maintain my equilibrium, but I have regained my self-esteem and now have a place to call home."

We, the Task Force on Homelessness and Severe Mental Illness, are certain that successes like these can become the rule, not the exception. We have outlined a way to reverse the tragic circumstances of homeless mentally ill Americans by marshalling the resources, knowledge, and leadership available in Federal, State, and local governments and in private organizations.

We foresee no quick fix to this complex national problem. Rather, we offer ideas and action steps that can catalyze an evolving national strategy to end homelessness among severely mentally ill individuals. The report says clearly: *This is a problem we can and must solve together. The time to begin is now.*

References

Advisory Commission on Regulatory Barriers to Affordable Housing. *"Not in My Back Yard": Removing Barriers to Affordable Housing*. Washington, DC: the Commission, 1991.

Allen, D.M.; Onorato, I.M.; and Wendell, D. "HIV Seroprevalence in Homeless Populations." Paper presented at the American Public Health Association Annual Convention, Atlanta, 1991.

Appelbaum, P.S. "Legal Issues Relevant to Homelessness and the Severely Mentally Ill Population." Unpublished paper prepared for the Task Force on Homelessness and Severe Mental Illness, 1991.

Bevilacqua, J.J. "Mental Illness in America: A Series of Public Hearings." Testimony presented at the National Advisory Mental Health Council and National Mental Health Leadership Forum Hearing on Severe Mental Illness and Homelessness, Chicago, 1991.

Breakey, W.R.; Fischer, P.J.; Kramer, M.; Nestadt G.; Romanoski, A.J.; Ross, A.; Royall, R.M.; and Stine, O.C. Health and mental health problems of homeless men and women in Baltimore. *Journal of the American Medical Association* 262(10):1352–1357, 1989.

Bricker, P. Clinical concerns in the care of homeless persons. In: Bricker, P., ed. *Under the Safety Net: The Health and Social Welfare of the Homeless in the United States*. New York: Norton, 1990.

Burt, M.R. Causes of the growth of homelessness during the 1980s. *Housing Policy Debate* 2(3):903–936, 1991.

Burt, M.R., and Cohen, B.E. *America's Homeless: Numbers, Characteristics, and the Programs that Serve Them*. Washington, DC: Urban Institute Press, 1989.

Chicago Coalition for the Homeless Mental Health Committee. "Chronic Mental Illness and Homelessness: Summary of Recommendations for Action." Testimony presented at the National Advisory Mental Health Council and National Mental Health Leadership Forum Hearing on Severe Mental Illness and Homelessness, Chicago, 1991.

Coalition for the Homeless and SRO Tenants Rights Coalition. *Single Room Occupancy Hotels: Standing in the Way of the Gentry*. New York: the Coalitions, 1985.

Crystal, S.; Ladner, S.; and Towber, C. Multiple impairment patterns in the mentally ill homeless. *International Journal of Mental Health* 14:61–73, 1985.

Dennis, D.L., and Steadman, H.J. "The Criminal Justice System and Severely Mentally Ill Homeless Persons: An Overview." Unpublished paper prepared for the Task Force on Homelessness and Severe Mental Illness, 1991.

Farr, R.; Koegel, P.; and Burman A. *A Study of Homelessness and Mental Illness in the Skid Row Area of Los Angeles*. Los Angeles: County Department of Mental Health, 1986.

Harp, H.T. "Mental Illness in America: A Series of Public Hearings." Testimony presented at the National Advisory Mental Health Council and National Mental Health Leadership Forum Hearing on Severe Mental Illness and Homelessness, Chicago, 1991.

Hopper, K. Symptoms, survival, and the redefinition of public space: A feasibility study of homeless people at a metropolitan airport. *Urban Anthropology* 20(2):155–175, 1991.

Institute of Medicine Committee on Health Care for Homeless People. *Homelessness, Health, and Human Needs*. Washington, DC: National Academy Press, 1988.

Interagency Council on the Homeless. *The 1990 Annual Report of the Interagency Council on the Homeless*. Washington, DC: the Council, 1991.

Judd, L.L. Putting mental health on the nation's health agenda. *Hospital and Community Psychiatry* 41(2):131–134, 1990.

Koyanagi, C., and Goldman, H.H. The quiet success of the national plan for the chronically mentally ill. *Hospital and Community Psychiatry* 42(9):899–905, 1991.

Lamb, H.R., ed. *The Homeless Mentally Ill: A Task Force Report of the American Psychiatric Association*. Washington, DC: American Psychiatric Association, 1984.

Levine, I.S. Service programs for the homeless mentally ill. In: Lamb, H.R., ed. *The Homeless Mentally Ill: A Task Force Report of the American Psychiatric Association*. Washington, DC: American Psychiatric Association, 1984.

Moran, M. Innovative program for homeless provides continuum of services in homelike setting. *Psychiatric News* 27(1):7, 1992.

Mulkern, V.; Bradley, V.; Spencer, R.; Allein, S.; and Oldham, J. *Homelessness Needs Assessment Study: Findings and Recommendations for the Massachusetts Department of Mental Health*. Boston: Human Services Research Institute, 1985.

Mulkern, V.M., and Manderscheid, R.W. Characteristics of community support program clients in 1980 and 1984. *Hospital and Community Psychiatry* 40(2):165–172, 1989.

The National Alliance to End Homelessness. *What You Can Do to Help the Homeless*. New York: Simon & Schuster, 1991.

National Mental Health Association and Families for the Homeless. *Homeless in America*. Washington, DC: Acropolis Books, 1988.

National Institute on Alcohol Abuse and Alcoholism. *Synopses of Community Dem-onstration Projects for Alcohol and Other Drug Abuse Treatment of Homeless Individuals.* Rockville, MD: the Institute, 1988.

National Institute on Alcohol Abuse and Alcoholism. *Synopses of Cooperative Agreements for Research Demonstration Projects on Alcohol and Other Drug Abuse Treatment for Homeless Persons.* DHHS Pub. No. (ADM)91–1763. Washington, DC: Supt. of Docs., U.S. Govt. Print. Off., 1991.

National Institute on Alcohol Abuse and Alcoholism. *Housing Initiatives for Home-less People with Alcohol and Other Drug Problems: Proceedings of a National Conference.* DHHS Pub. No. (ADM)92–1885. Washington, DC: Supt. of Docs., U.S. Govt. Print. Off., 1992.

National Institute of Mental Health. *Two Generations of NIMH-Funded Research on Homelessness and Mental Illness: 1982–1990.* Rockville, MD: the Institute, 1991*a*.

National Institute of Mental Health. *Additions and Resident Patients at End of Year, State and County Mental Hospitals, by Age and Diagnosis, by State, United States, 1989.* Rockville, MD: the Institute, 1991*b*.

National Institute of Mental Health. *Caring for People with Severe Mental Disorders: A National Plan of Research to Improve Services.* DHHS Pub. No. (ADM)91–1762. Washington, DC: Supt. of Docs., U.S. Govt. Print. Off., 1991*c*.

Newman, S.J. "The Severely Mentally Ill Homeless: Housing Needs and Housing Policy." Unpublished paper prepared for the U.S. Department of Housing and Urban Development, 1991.

Notkin, S.; Rosenthal, B.; and Hopper, K. *Families on the Move: Breaking the Cycle of Homelessness.* New York: Edna McConnell Clark Foundation, 1990.

President's Commission on Mental Health. *Report to the President from the President's Commission on Mental Health.* Washington, DC: Supt. of Docs., U.S. Govt. Print. Off., 1978.

Rabasca, L. Winter brings homeless to New York's subways. *Mental Health Report* 16(1):2, 1992.

Surles, R.; Feiden-Warsh, C.; and Hopper, K. "A White Paper on Components of A Comprehensive System to Address Homelessness Among the Severely Men-tally Ill." Unpublished paper prepared for the Task Force on Homelessness and Severe Mental Illness, 1991.

Susser, E.S.; Lin S.P.; Conover, S.A.; and Struening, E.L. Childhood antecedents of homelessness in psychiatric patients. *American Journal of Psychiatry* 148(8):1026–1030, 1991.

Tessler, R.C., and Dennis, D.L. *A Synthesis of NIMH-Funded Research Concerning Persons Who Are Homeless and Mentally Ill.* Rockville, MD: National Institute of Mental Health, 1989.

U.S. Congress, House Committee on Government Operations. *The Federal Role in Providing Services to the Mentally Ill.* Hearing Before the Subcommittee on Human Resources and Intergovernmental Relations. Washington, DC: Supt. of Docs., U.S. Govt. Print. Off., May 19, 1987.

U.S. Congress. *Mental Health Systems Act.* Public Law 96–398, Oct. 1980.

U.S. Department of Health and Human Services Steering Committee on the Chronically Mentally Ill. *Toward a National Plan for the Chronically Mentally Ill.* Washington, DC: the Department, 1980.

U.S. Department of Health and Human Services. "The Homeless: Background, Analysis, and Options." Briefing paper prepared by the HHS Working Group on the Homeless and submitted to the U.S. House of Representatives Subcommittee on Intergovernmental Relations and Human Resources, Washington, DC, 1984.

U.S. General Accounting Office. *Returning the Mentally Disabled to the Community: Government Needs to Do More.* Washington, DC: Supt. of Docs., U.S. Govt. Print. Off., 1977.

Van Tosh, L. "Mental Illness in America: A Series of Public Hearings." Testimony presented at the National Advisory Mental Health Council and National Mental Health Leadership Forum Hearing on Severe Mental Illness and Homelessness, Chicago, 1991.

Appendix

Advisory Committee Members

Edward Brandt, M.D., Ph.D.
Executive Dean
College of Medicine
University of Oklahoma Health Sciences
     Center
Oklahoma City, Oklahoma

William R. Breakey, M.D.*
Director
Community Psychiatry Program
Department of Psychiatry and Behavioral
     Sciences
The Johns Hopkins Medical Institutions
Baltimore, Maryland

Paul C. Brophy
Vice Chair
Enterprise Foundation
Columbia, Maryland

June Jackson Christmas, M.D.
Clinical Professor of Psychiatry
Columbia University College of
     Physicians and Surgeons
New York, New York

Nancy Domenici
Advocate for People with Mental Illness
New Mexico/Washington, D.C.

Laurie Flynn
Executive Director
National Alliance for the Mentally Ill
Arlington, Virginia

Jana Graves
Director
Embry-Rucker Shelter
Reston, Virginia

Kim Hopper, Ph.D.
Research Scientist, Nathan Kline Institute
     for Psychiatric Research
President, National Coalition for the
     Homeless
Orangeburg, New York

Teh-wei Hu, Ph.D.
Professor of Health Economics
School of Public Health
University of California at Berkeley
Berkeley, California

Beverly H. Robinson, Ph.D., R.N.
Assistant Professor
University of Texas Health Science
     Center
San Antonio School of Nursing
San Antonio, Texas

Miles Shore, M.D.
Director
Program on Mental Illness
Robert Wood Johnson Foundation
Boston, Massachusetts

Richard Surles, Ph.D.
Commissioner
New York State Office of Mental Health
Albany, New York

Henry R. Tarke, L.C.S.W.
Central Regional Manager
San Diego County
     Mental Health Services
San Diego, California

Michael B. Unhjem, J.D.
President
Blue Cross/Blue Shield of North Dakota
Fargo, North Dakota

Laura Van Tosh
Policy Associate
Mental Health Policy Studies
Department of Psychiatry
University of Maryland
Baltimore, Maryland

Chauncey Veatch III, J.D.
Alcohol and Drug Abuse Treatment
     Consultant
Sacramento, California

---

* Replaced John Talbott, M.D., who resigned on July 1, 1991 due to sabbatical leave.

Federal Staff

Task Force Staff

Jane Steinberg, Ph.D.
Staff Director *
Task Force on Homelessness and
   Severe Mental Illness

Catherine V. Tall, M.S.W.
Public Health Analyst
Task Force on Homelessness and
   Severe Mental Illness

Margie Ritter
Program Assistant
Task Force on Homelessness and
   Severe Mental Illness

Senior Advisors

Irene S. Levine, Ph.D.
Director
Office of Programs for the Homeless
   Mentally Ill
National Institute of Mental Health
Department of Health and Human
   Services

Fred C. Osher, M.D.
Deputy Director
Office of Programs for the Homeless
   Mentally Ill
National Institute of Mental Health
Department of Health and Human
   Services

James Forsberg
Director
Office of Special Needs Assistance
   Programs
Department of Housing and Urban
   Development

Michael Jewell
Program Analyst
Office of the Assistant Secretary for
   Planning and Evaluation
Department of Health and Human
   Services

Writer

Anne Rosenfeld
Public Affairs Specialist
Office of the Director
National Institute of Mental Health
Department of Health and Human
   Services

Typist

Patricia Godwin
Secretary
Office of Programs for the Homeless
   Mentally Ill
National Institute of Mental Health
Department of Health and Human
   Services

Departmental Staff

Bernard Arons, M.D.
Chief
System Development and Community
   Support Branch
National Institute of Mental Health
Department of Health and Human
   Services

Richard Chambers
Director
Office of Intergovernmental Affairs
Health Care Financing Administration
Department of Health and Human
   Services

Terrlyn Curry, M.A.
Research Psychologist
Office of Programs for the Homeless
   Mentally Ill
National Institute of Mental Health
Department of Health and Human
   Services

Paul Errera, M.D.
Director
Mental Health and Behavioral Sciences
   Service
Department of Veterans Affairs

---

* Replaced Barry Blackwell, M.D., who served as Staff Director from December 1990 through May 1991.

Elaine Fraser
Clerk
Office of Programs for the Homeless
    Mentally Ill
National Institute of Mental Health
Department of Health and Human
    Services

Paul Hancock
Chief
Housing and Civil Enforcement Section
Civil Rights Division
Department of Justice

John Heinberg
Chief
Evaluation Unit
Division of Performance, Management
    and Evaluation
Department of Labor

Marsha Henderson
Director of Monitoring and Evaluation
Interagency Council on the Homeless

Ann Hohmann, Ph.D.
Health Science Administrator
Services Research Branch
National Institute of Mental Health
Department of Health and Human
    Services

Robert Huebner, Ph.D.
Acting Chief
Homeless Demonstration and Evaluation
    Branch
National Institute on Alcohol Abuse and
    Alcoholism
Department of Health and Human
    Services

Mark Johnston
Deputy Director
Office of Special Needs Assistance
    Programs
Department of Housing and Urban
    Development

Bryan Keilty
Deputy Administrator
Office of Strategic Planning and Policy
    Development
Employment and Training Administration
Department of Labor

Cille Kennedy, Ph.D.
Psychologist
Services Research Branch
National Institute of Mental Health
Department of Health and Human
    Services

Darrell Kirch, M.D.
Deputy Director
Division of Clinical Research
National Institute of Mental Health
Department of Health and Human
    Services

Eric Lindblom, J.D.
Homelessness Policy Analyst
Department of Veterans Affairs

Kathryn Magruder, Ph.D., M.P.H.
Assistant Chief
Services Research Branch
National Institute of Mental Health
Department of Health and Human
    Services

Ronald Manderscheid, Ph.D.
Chief
Statistical Research Branch
National Institute of Mental Health
Department of Health and Human
    Services

Robin Michaelson
Public Health Analyst
Office of Programs for the Homeless
    Mentally Ill
National Institute of Mental Health
Department of Health and Human
    Services

Peggy Murray
Public Health Analyst
Homeless Demonstration and Evaluation
    Branch
National Institute on Alcohol Abuse and
    Alcoholism
Department of Health and Human
    Services

Grayson Norquist, M.D., M.S.P.H.
Deputy Director
Division of Applied and Services
    Research
National Institute of Mental Health
Department of Health and Human
    Services

Katherine Olberg
PATH Program Director
Office of Programs for the Homeless
  Mentally Ill
National Institute of Mental Health
Department of Health and Human
  Services

Eileen Pederson
Manpower Analyst
Office of Strategic Planning and Policy
  Development
Employment and Training Administration
Department of Labor

Eileen Penner, J.D.
Attorney
Housing and Civil Enforcement Section
Department of Justice

Frances Randolph, Ph.D.
Public Health Advisor
Systems Development and Community
  Support Branch
National Institute of Mental Health
Department of Health and Human
  Services

Connie Reiter
Program Assistant
Office of the Assistant Secretary for
  Planning and Evaluation
Department of Health and Human
  Services

Agnes Rupp, Ph.D.
Economist
Services Research Branch
National Institute of Mental Health
Department of Health and Human
  Services

Peter Spencer
Deputy Associate Commissioner
Office of Supplemental Security Income
Social Security Administration
Department of Health and Human
  Services

Sharman Stephens
Program Analyst
Office of the Assistant Secretary for
  Planning and Evaluation
Department of Health and Human
  Services

Roger Straw, Ph.D.
Associate Director of Research
Office of Programs for the Homeless
  Mentally Ill
National Institute of Mental Health
Department of Health and Human
  Services

Suzanne Tillman
Vocational Rehabilitation Program
  Specialist
Rehabilitation Services Administration
Department of Education

Perry Vietti
Special Needs Assistance Specialist
Office of Special Needs Assistance
  Programs
Department of Housing and Urban
  Development

Ecford Voit, Ph.D.
Assistant Chief
Violence and Traumatic Stress Research
  Branch
National Institute of Mental Health
Department of Health and Human
  Services

Jean Whaley
Assistant Director for Program
  Development
Office of Special Needs Assistance
  Programs
Department of Housing and Urban
  Development

Susan Young
Policy Analyst
Office of the Assistant Secretary for
  Planning and Evaluation
Department of Health and Human
  Services

Participants in Special Issue Meetings

Meeting on Housing Issues—June 17, 1991

James Forsberg, Co-Chair
Director
Office of Special Needs Assistance
    Programs
Department of Housing and Urban
    Development

Irene S. Levine, Ph.D., Co-Chair
Director
Office of Programs for the Homeless
    Mentally Ill
National Institute of Mental Health
Department of Health and Human
    Services

Martin Cohen, M.S.W.
Program on Mental Illness
Robert Wood Johnson Foundation
Boston, Massachusetts

Cushing Dolbeare
Consultant on Housing and Public Policy
Washington, D.C.

Betsy Morris
Assistant Executive Director
San Diego Housing Commission
San Diego, California

Emilie Murphy
New York Program Director
Corporation for Supportive Housing
New York, New York

Sandra Newman, Ph.D.
Associate Director for Research
Institute for Policy Studies
The Johns Hopkins University
Baltimore, Maryland

Steven Pines
Director, Housing Plus
Enterprise Foundation
Baltimore, Maryland

Julie Sandorf
President
Corporation for Supportive Housing
New York, New York

Meeting on State Mental Health Authority Housing Issues—June 26, 1991

Danna Mauch, Ph.D., Chair
PDM Health Strategies
Cambridge, Massachusetts

Laurie Curtis
Technical Assistance Specialist
The Center for Community Change
Burlington, Vermont

Ann Denton
Coordinator of Housing and Residential
    Services
Texas Department of Mental Health and
    Mental Retardation
Austin, Texas

Beth R. Edgar
Housing Specialist
Vermont Department of Mental Health
Waterbury, Vermont

Joseph Manes
Director of Government Relations
Mental Health Law Project
Washington, D.C.

Bonnie Millstein
Director of Community Watch
Mental Health Law Project
Washington, D.C.

Henry Pierson III
Project Coordinator
South Carolina Department of Mental
    Health
Columbia, South Carolina

E. Clarke Ross, D.P.A.
Assistant Executive Director for Federal
    Relations
National Association of State Mental
    Health Program Directors
Washington, D.C.

Sam Shull
Housing Coordinator
Virginia Department of Mental Health,
    Mental Retardation and Substance
    Abuse Services
Richmond, Virginia

Meeting on Minority Issues—July 24, 1991

June Jackson Christmas, M.D., Chair
Department of Psychiatry
Columbia University College of
    Physicians and Surgeons
New York, New York

Susanna Chan, M.Ed.
Director of Mental Health
South Cove Community Health Center
Boston, Massachusetts

Sydney Donaville
Research Associate
Center for Self-Help Research
Berkeley, California

Carol Hernandez, Ph.D.
Assistant Deputy Director for the
    Northeast Area
Ohio Department of Mental Health
Columbus, Ohio

Mary Long, R.N.
Vice President of Government Affairs
Arthritis Foundation
Atlanta, Georgia

Margarita Lopez, M.S.W.
Team Leader
Project Reachout
New York, New York

Marsha Martin, D.S.W.
Associate Professor
Hunter College School of Social Work
New York, New York

Harriet McCombs, Ph.D.
Research Director
Columbia Area Mental Health Center
Columbia, South Carolina

Amy Okamura
Program Manager
Union of Pan Asian Communities
San Diego, California

Altha J. Stewart, M.D.
Deputy Commissioner for Program
    Services
New York City Department of Mental
    Health, Mental Retardation, and
    Alcoholism
New York, New York

Grace H. Stuckey, M.S.W.
Homelessness Services Coordinator
Virginia Department of Mental Health,
    Mental Retardation and Substance
    Abuse Services
Richmond, Virginia

Phyllis Wolfe
Director of the D.C. Project
Children's Defense Fund
Washington, D.C.

Meeting on Consumer Issues—August 19, 1991

Laura Van Tosh, Chair
Coordinator *
The National Mental Health Consumer
    Self-Help Clearinghouse
Philadelphia, Pennsylvania

John Allen
Executive Director
On Our Own Computer Center
Rockville, Maryland

William Brown
Share Your Bounty
Bronx, New York

William Butler
Collaborative Service Programs of New
    Jersey
Freehold, New Jersey

Woody Cade
Friends Helping Friends
Nashville, Tennessee

Judi Chamberlain
Teleconference Coordinator
Center for Psychiatric Rehabilitation
Boston University
Boston, Massachusetts

Diane Coté
Project Administrator
PEOPLe
Poughkeepsie, New York

Chris Gray
Transportation Technician 2
Washington State Department of
    Transportation
Seattle, Washington

Jacki McKinney
Director of Consumer Case Management
Project Share
Philadelphia, Pennsylvania

David Ogden
Consumer Outreach Worker
Money and Mailboxes
Cleveland, Ohio

Veronica Pearson
Oakland Independence Support Center
Oakland, California

---

* Currently Policy Associate, Mental Health Policy Studies, Department of Psychiatry, University of Maryland.

Meeting on Rehabilitation Issues—September 12, 1991

Richard Surles, Ph.D., Chair
Commissioner
New York State Office of Mental Health
Albany, New York

John Allen
Executive Director
On Our Own Computer Center
Rockville, Maryland

William Anthony, Ph.D.
Director and Professor
Center for Psychiatric Rehabilitation
Boston University
Boston, Massachusetts

Sara Asmussen, Ph.D.
Director of Research
Fountain House
New York, New York

Judith A. Cook, Ph.D.
Director
Thresholds National Research and
    Training Center
Chicago, Illinois

Susan Dempsay
Executive Director
Step-Up-On-Second
Santa Monica, California

Cynthia Feiden-Warsh
Director of Operations
New York State Office of Mental Health
Albany, New York

Benjamin Gross
Vice President
Argus Community, Inc.
Bronx, New York

Tony Hannigan, M.S.W.
Executive Director
Columbia University Community Services
New York, New York

Ruth A. Hughes, Ph.D.
Executive Director
International Association of Psychosocial
    Rehabilitation Services
Columbia, Maryland

Judith Johnson
Director
The Green Door
Washington, D.C.

Laura Mancuso, M.S., C.R.C.
Director of Technical Assistance
National Association of State Mental
    Health Program Directors
Alexandria, Virginia

Irvin D. Rutman, Ph.D.
President
Matrix Research Institute
Philadelphia, Pennsylvania

Jerome Vaccaro, M.D.
Assistant Chief
Rehabilitation Medicine Services
Veterans Administration Medical Center
    West Los Angeles
Los Angeles, California

Steven Warren
Executive Director
Services for the Underserved
New York, New York

Linda Zelch
Deputy Director for Program Development
Ohio Department of Mental Health
Columbus, Ohio

Meeting on Legal Issues—September 20, 1991

Michael Unhjem, J.D., Chair
President
Blue Cross/Blue Shield of North Dakota
Fargo, North Dakota

Paul Appelbaum, M.D.
Professor
Department of Psychiatry
University of Massachusetts Medical
    Center
Worcester, Massachusetts

William Breakey, M.D.
Director
Community Psychiatry Program
Department of Psychiatry and Behavioral
    Sciences
The Johns Hopkins Medical Institutions
Baltimore, Maryland

Jay Centifanti, J.D., M.B.A.
Deputy Director
Pennsylvania Protection and Advocacy
Harrisburg, Pennsylvania

Linda Chafetz, R.N., DNSc.
Associate Professor
Department of Mental Health, Community
    and Administrative Nursing
University of California, San Francisco
San Francisco, California

Miguel Chavez, M.S.W.
Senior Advocate
Protection and Advocacy System
Las Vegas, New Mexico

Areta Crowell, Ph.D.
Local Mental Health Director
San Diego County Department of Health
    Services
San Diego, California

Deborah Dennis, M.A.
Project Director
National Resource Center on
    Homelessness and Mental Illness
Delmar, New York

Loretta Haggard
Intern
Legal Services of Eastern Missouri
St. Louis, Missouri

Ron Honberg, J.D.
Legislative Liaison
National Alliance for the Mentally Ill
Arlington, Virginia

John Horner
President
National Mental Health Association
Alexandria, Virginia

Arlene Kanter, J.D.
Director of Clinical Programs
Syracuse University College of Law
Syracuse, New York

Ingo Keilitz, J.D.
Director
Institute on Mental Disabilities and the
    Law
National Center for State Courts
Williamsburg, Virginia

Robert T.M. Phillips, M.D., Ph.D.
Director
Whiting Forensic Institute
Middletown, Connecticut

Leonard Rubenstein, J.D.
Director
Mental Health Law Project
Washington, D.C.

Michael M. Scimeca, M.D.
Director
Montefiore/Rikers Island Mental Health
    Services
East Elmhurst, New York

Richard Sheola
Senior Assistant Vice President for
    Mental Health Services
New York City Health and Hospitals
    Corporation
New York, New York

Larry Soloman
Deputy Director
National Institute of Corrections
Washington, D.C.

Henry J. Steadman, Ph.D.
President
Policy Research Associates, Inc.
Delmar, New York

Meeting on Evaluation Issues—December 16, 1991

Alan I. Leshner, Ph.D., Chair
Chair, Task Force on Homelessness and
    Severe Mental Illness
Acting Director, National Institute of
    Mental Health
Department of Health and Human
    Services

Susan Essock, Ph.D.
Director of Psychological Services
Connecticut Department of Mental Health
Hartford, Connecticut

Howard Goldman, M.D., Ph.D.
Professor
Department of Psychiatry
University of Maryland
Baltimore, Maryland

William Hargreaves, Ph.D.
Professor of Medical Psychology
Department of Psychiatry
University of California at San Francisco

Sandra Newman, Ph.D.
Associate Director for Research
The Johns Hopkins Institute for Policy
    Studies
Baltimore, Maryland

Donald M. Steinwachs, Ph.D.
Director
Health Services Research and
    Development Center
The Johns Hopkins University
Baltimore, Maryland

Organizational Contributors

The Task Force on Homelessness and Severe Mental Illness would like to thank the many organizations that contributed advice, convened or participated in meetings, or prepared position papers to facilitate its efforts. Acknowledgment in the list below signifies our appreciation, not the organization's endorsement of this document.

Alliance for the Mentally Ill - Maryland Chapter
Alliance for the Mentally Ill - New York Chapter
American Academy of Child and Adolescent Psychiatry
American Association for Counseling and Development
American Association for Marriage and Family Therapy
American Association for Partial Hospitalization
American Association of Retired Persons
American Psychiatric Association
American Psychological Association
American Psychological Society
American Public Welfare Association
Anxiety Disorders Association of America
Argus Community, Inc.
Arthritis Foundation
Blue Cross/Blue Shield of North Dakota
Boston University Center for Psychiatric Rehabilitation
Catholic Charities USA
Center for Self-Help Research
The Center for Community Change through Housing and Support
Child Welfare League of America
Children's Defense Fund
Council of Large Public Housing Authorities
Collaborative Service Programs of New Jersey
Columbia Area Mental Health Center
Columbia University College of Physicians and Surgeons
Columbia University Community Services
Connecticut Department of Mental Health
Connecticut Veterans Affairs Medical Center
Corporation for Supportive Housing
Council of State Community Development Agencies
Enterprise Foundation

Federation of Behavioral, Psychological, and Cognitive Sciences
Fountain House
Friends Helping Friends
Goodwill Industries of America, Inc.
The Green Door
Home Builders Institute
Hunter College School of Social Work
International Association of Psychosocial Rehabilitation Services
The Johns Hopkins University Health Services Research and Development Center
The Johns Hopkins University Institute for Policy Studies
The Johns Hopkins University Department of Psychiatry and Behavioral Sciences
Legal Action Center
Legal Services of Eastern Missouri
Matrix Research Institute
Mental Health Law Project
Mental Health Policy Resource Center
Money and Mailboxes
Montefiore/Rikers Island Mental Health Services
Nathan Kline Institute for Psychiatric Research
National Alliance for the Mentally Ill
National Alliance to End Homelessness
National Association of Area Agencies on Aging
National Association of Counties
National Association of Housing and Redevelopment Officials
National Association of Protection and Advocacy Systems
National Association of State Alcohol and Drug Abuse Directors
National Association of State Mental Health Program Directors
National Center for State Courts
National Coalition for the Homeless
National Conference of State Legislatures

National Council of Community Mental Health Centers
National Law Center on Homelessness and Poverty
National League of Cities
National Low Income Housing Coalition
National Mental Health Association
National Mental Health Consumer Self-Help Clearinghouse
National Resource Center on Homelessness and Mental illness
National Senior Citizens Law Center
National Urban League, Inc.
New Hampshire Division of Mental Health and Developmental Services
New Mexico Protection and Advocacy System
New York City Department of Mental Health, Mental Retardation, and Alcoholism Services
New York City Health and Hospitals Corporation
New York City Human Resources Administration
New York State Office of Mental Health
Oakland Independence Support Center
Ohio Department of Mental Health
On Our Own Computer Center
PDM Health Strategies
Pennsylvania Protection and Advocacy System
PEOPLe
Policy Research Associates, Inc.
Project Reachout
Project SHARE
Robert Wood Johnson Foundation
San Diego County Department of Health Services

San Diego Housing Commission
Services for the Underserved
Share Your Bounty
South Carolina Department of Mental Health
South Cove Community Health Center
Step-Up-On-Second
Syracuse University College of Law
Texas Department of Mental Health and Mental Retardation
Thresholds National Research and Training Center
Travelers' Aid International
Union of Pan Asian Communities
United Way of America
University of California at San Francisco, Department of Mental Health, Community and Administrative Nursing
University of California at San Francisco, Department of Psychiatry
University of Maryland Mental Health Policy Studies
University of Massachusetts Department of Psychiatry
U.S. Conference of Mayors
Vermont Department of Mental Health
Veterans Administration Medical Center, W. Los Angeles
Virginia Department of Mental Health, Mental Retardation and Substance Abuse Services
Washington Legal Clinic for the Homeless, Inc.
Washington State Department of Transportation
Whiting Forensic Institute

Acronyms

ACCESS	Access to Community Care and Effective Services and Supports
ADA	Americans with Disabilities Act
ADAMHA	Alcohol, Drug Abuse, and Mental Health Administration, PHS, HHS
ADMS	Alcohol, Drug Abuse, and Mental Health Services Block Grant
AIDS	Acquired Immunodeficiency Syndrome
CMHC	Community Mental Health Center
DOEd	Department of Education
DOJ	Department of Justice
DOL	Department of Labor
FHAA	Fair Housing Amendments Act of 1988
HHS	Department of Health and Human Services
HCFA	Health Care Financing Administration, HHS
HCMI	Homeless Chronically Mentally Ill Veterans Program, VA
HIV	Human Immunodeficiency Virus
HUD	Department of Housing and Urban Development
JTPA	Job Training Partnership Act
NIAAA	National Institute on Alcohol Abuse and Alcoholism, ADAMHA, PHS, HHS
NIMBY	Not In My Back Yard
NIMH	National Institute of Mental Health, ADAMHA, PHS, HHS
PATH	Projects for Assistance in Transition from Homelessness, NIMH, ADAMHA, HHS
PHA	Public Housing Authority
PHS	Public Health Service, HHS
S+C	Shelter Plus Care
SRO	Single Room Occupancy
SSA	Social Security Administration, HHS
SSDI	Supplemental Security Disability Insurance, SSA, HHS
SSI	Supplemental Security Income, SSA, HHS
USDA	Department of Agriculture
VA	Department of Veterans Affairs